Be It H̶nble

A dialogue at the threshold of Family, Ancestors, Culture and Home

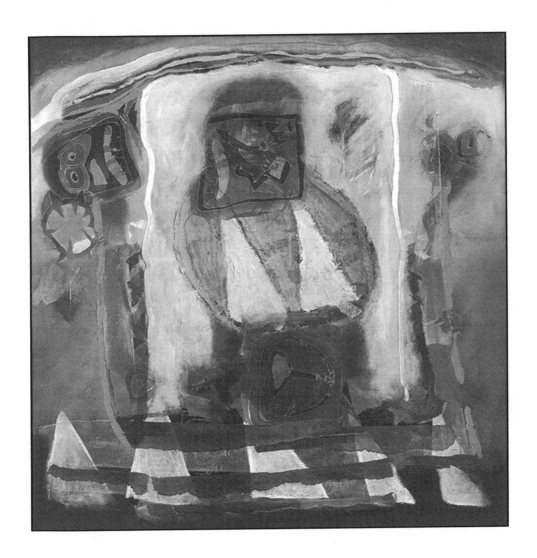

Jerome Kerner

ISBN: 1-4392-5142-8
ISBN-13: 9781439251423

Visit www.booksurge.com to order additional copies.

Acknowledgments

I would like to express my gratitude to those who had an indirect influence on this book, teachers who helped me to discover that I have an inner life, an authentic self that has a voice, including: Eva and Dr. John Pierakos, John Saly (The Pathwork), Dr. Ed Lynch (Southern Conn. State Univ.Gestalt training), Bert Hellinger, Susan and John Ulfelder (Hellinger D.C.), Dr. Alexis Johnson and Dr. Judith Schmidt (Center for Intentional Living).

As I found my voice and the book emerged, the editing and encouragement from Suzi Tucker were invaluable to me and the process of completing the work.

Finally, the deep and unconditional love I receive from my wife and partner Alexis is a constant source of encouragement and inspiration. The home environment that we have created together is a reflection of both our families and of the mutual love we share.

Contents

Prologue

As we prepare to go to press with this book the global economy is in crisis. A crisis brought on by three things; excessive borrowing, the lack of regulation of lending, and the notion that "money is king". During this period of expansion two facts were evident; first, the gap between haves and have not's increased, and second, the haves kept raising the bar for the defining of wealth. Wealth, money itself was used as a way of defining our success rather than the products of our labor, ideas, innovations or service that might benefit our society. This new wealth was flaunted in acquiring bigger homes, bigger cars and a larger than life lifestyle. If some acted as though money was limitless, that attitude also carried over into the environment and our natural resources.

This lifestyle paradigm was a big shift from that of the previous decade when our grandparents immigrated to the United States with little or nothing and brought with them the values of generations before. These values which placed family and community above personal gain served them well during the transition to the "new world" and later thru The Great War, a depression and The Second World War.

Frank Rich in a recent Op Ed column in the New York Times quotes The grandfather in the Clifford Odets classic drama of the Great Depression *Awake and Sing* "Boychick, wake up!" the Grandfather Jacob tells his Grandson, Ralph, as the battered Berger family disintegrates in the Bronx. "Be something! Make your life something good....go out and fight so life shouldn't be printed on dollar bills."

It is time now to redefine abundance and the ways in which we will define ourselves. In the process of doing so we can benefit by revisiting the ethos of our ancestors, their higher values, those values that contributed to their survival (and yes, their thriving) through difficult times.

If you believe as I do that something positive can be taken away from even the most distressful situation, then perhaps the redefining of abundance, learning who we are in relationship to the past, can be the positive aspect of the current economic crisis. As Walter Lippmann said, "Men can know more than their ancestors did if they start with a knowledge of what their ancestors had already learned….That is why a society can be progressive only if it preserves it's traditions."

Preface

Be It Ever So Humble is not a book to be read rapidly. It is a book that invites the reader to challenge sensory experiences and to actively reach deep into lost memories. The result of this exercise can be a positive experience filled with insights. To actively participate in the exercises, the reader must be willing to be in the here and now while bridging time and space to connect with family, ancestors and culture. The book creates a way to access our inner unconscious voices, and by having a dialogue with those voices we can better understand our actions toward creating our living space. In addition to the dialogues, the reader is asked to draw upon personal memories or dreams that we associate with living spaces during our early development and that of the generations before us.

As an architect, Mr. Kerner has spent his life working with structure to create space. However, his interests are well beyond the aesthetics of design and focus more on the subliminal, unconscious and emotional experience of space. His interests in family systems and trans-generational impact provide an alternative explanation of how we experience space. Perhaps the most intriguing aspect of the book is how, as we have confused large structures with success, we have reduced the pleasant opportunities for humans to socially interact and to use each other as "regulators" in a challenging world. Specifically, we have created living structures that instead of supporting needed privacy have resulted in behaviors of secrecy and the consequential experiences of isolation and alienation. In a sense we have responded to our desires to be "in fashion" and have neglected our biological need to relate interpersonally and to feel safe. Conversely, we may be following an old family pattern unconsciously, playing out old negative patterns out of a sense of loyalty, when there may be a healthier way to express that loyalty.

As we re-experience the memories of our childhood and attempt to experience the "space" of our ancestors, we start to understand our personal needs for and benefits of affiliation. We start to realize that the physical space that we proudly construct may provide limitations on our interpersonal experiences, our ability to parent, our ability to be a loving spouse, our ability to entertain, and even our ability to be creative and to feel benevolent. Thus, we realize that the space we design must fit well with our personal quest for safety and privacy, while understanding that the decisions we make are grounded in the acceptance or rejection of the ways of our family, ancestors and culture and that whichever the case, we are better off doing so consciously.

Mr. Kerner has evoked the doorway as a metaphor for the way we move through our lives. *Be It Ever So Humble* may be one of those "doorways". Metaphorically, the cover is a door that may be voluntarily opened to experience a new way of seeing the home.

Please open the book and venture into the unique experience that Mr. Kerner offers.

Stephen W. Porges, Ph.D.
Director, Brain-Body Center
Department of Psychiatry
University of Illinois at Chicago

The Basics

ARCHOLOGIE: BE IT EVER SO HUMBLE
A dialogue at the threshold of family, ancestors, culture and home.

We are all at the threshold
Always at the threshold
Entering or leaving
Indecisively
One leg in one leg out
Wanting both
Inevitably we must step through.
Inside we are embraced by walls
These become memories or blank surfaces
On which we project images, real or imagined
We can experience this as a magical journey
Or as the fun house of distorted mirrors
Or as a reflection of our inner world with all it's imperfections.

Or

We can stay out
And live with the nagging wonder of what might be discovered inside.
What nugget of ore might be found.
And in finding it could make this a life.
And what is a life without self-discovery.

Much of our life is spent learning what is and what is not acceptable behavior. We learn how to address others and how to dress ourselves, and often we simply follow the latest trends in fashion and décor. Why do we do this? Is our desire to be accepted and approved of so strong that it overrides our inner voice?

1

When Carl Jung spoke of the "collective unconscious" he referred to an instinctive conformity to tribal and cultural archetypal behavior and ways of being. Through the process of assimilation, we leave our group of origin and as we do we join new groups, often of a diverse composition.

The term "Groupthink" introduced in the 1950's was discovered as a symptom through the process called Focus Groups employed by industry to evaluate new products and ideas. Groupthink could be seen as rationalized conformity in an attempt to avoid controversy, or simply not to appear foolish, rather than the instinctive conformity that keeps us safe from grave consequences of nonconforming, such as excommunication or execution.

Often the new group that forms will have many common aspects, but the critical common denominator may ultimately be our family of origin and cultural influences that stem from those relationships, both actual and phenomenological.

These relationships to family and culture can be subtle and in the rush to assimilate in order to survive in a new environment, family and culture are subordinated and often forgotten, making it difficult to reconnect.

However, reconnection is possible and essential. It can occur thru dreams, imagery and gestalt experiments, all of which will be a part of this personal process workbook.

Participating fully in the exercises will allow you to momentarily observe the intuitive decisions alongside of rational decisions, and, in so doing you can then make a conscious choice as to which approach will give you the most accurate and creative expression of who you are today. It is important to remember that these same questions will be dealt with by your offspring, and maintaining the thread will be a gift to them in their process of self-discovery.

This book will ask you to reflect on your current living space and how accurately it represents who you are today. Together we will appraise and reflect on the current space to help you see where your developed and undeveloped aspects are being reinforced by that space.

I will offer exercises that will allow you to see for yourself where there are inconsistencies between self and reflection. You will discover needs that can be addressed right now that will set a direction for the future.

We will explore together the process of becoming aware of the subliminal influences on our personal space, on our home.

The process itself can be transformational one. Carl Jung has been quoted as saying, "The work in progress becomes the Poet's fate and determines his psychic development. It is not Goethe that creates Faust, but Faust which creates Goethe."

The approach we will use is both personal and phenomenological; that is, responding to your space by having a dialogue with it, and allowing your immediate reactions to and from the space to be heard. You will be asked to be attentive to dream states, both awake and asleep, and to follow projective techniques, i.e., "Rorscach-like drawings," to assist in the discovery process that will lead to the design that responds to your need.

In order to have this dialogue you must become aware of your emotional reaction to your space. To quote Fritz Perls, the father of gestalt therapy, "The emotions are the life of us, the very language of the organism."

When you look at your living space through the lens of your emotional reaction to that space, what happens? What arises in you? If the answer is nothing much, that should give you plenty to work with. On the other hand, if you allow yourself to reflect on "know thyself" and finding the "genre de vie," you may find the critical building blocks that form a more responsible way of creating your home.

Response-ability as defined here is the ability to respond to what arises in you as you participate in the process, in the exercises I will suggest. It is your willingness to respond to your inner voices, as well as the voices of others within you and the voices of external objects as well.

This is not an easy process to undertake. There are inhibitions to creating the right space, such as memories of the past, financial restrictions of the present, and the ever-present need to compromise to keep peace in the family.

The key is to commit yourself to change through a new awareness. If you are committed to change, there will be a ripple effect throughout your life and throughout your family.

The concept of being a Witness to your inner voices and your reactions to them will come up again and again in the book. Similarly the concepts of Awareness,

Intentionality, Soul, and Loyalty will also recur. Therefore, I would like to take a moment here to define these terms, starting with the overarching concept of Archologie.

Archologie: The Overarching Concept

There is broad acceptance for the idea that family-tribal culture affects our spiritual beliefs, sexual attitudes (which include attitudes concerning privacy), and the way in which we relate to others. Family and tribal influences also affect how we create and inhabit our personal spaces, our homes. From the choice of natural or artificial light to be perceived by the eye, to the preference of temperature to be felt by the skin, to the attitudes we have about shared and communal space, values and preferences are shaped by many layers of history, seen and unseen.

Archologie is the active practice of remembering the family of origin, the ancestors, and the tribe, and the ways in which they created home and safety. Archologie becomes an active practice with the use of gestalt experiments, which allow us to give a voice to those not present as well as to inanimate objects and spaces. Archologie also uses guided visualizations and waking dreams to allow us to revisit or visit for the first time the homes of our ancestors to sense and feel how they created home. Upon returning from this journey, we have a heightened sense of our origins and therefore who we are. From this place we can make informed decisions about our own homes. I underscore the words *informed decisions* as opposed to change, because the objective is to become conscious of the influences that act upon us, not necessarily to change them. From this point of view, *history has a vote, not a veto.*

> Archologie should not be confused with Feng Shui, which is the art of becoming in harmony with your environment through an Eastern set of principles, related to Eastern cosmological beliefs that explain the flow of energy and a morally responsible way of building in the environment. Many Feng Shuei principles are good practice no matter what your belief system. However, employing these principles may bring a sense of peace or energetic flow, but if you ignore your inner voice, that is, the echo's of your psyche, this sense of peace and flow will not endure.

Archologie is particularly relevant for:
- People who are contemplating the design of a home
- People who are experiencing discomfort in their current home
- Therapists with clients who have exhibited a concern about their home
- Design professionals who would like to include Archologie in their practice

Keywords

Each of the keywords below relate to a section of the workbook in the same order that they appear here.

AWARENESS: *Am I present in the moment?*
Awareness as part of the process of Archologie refers to the here-and-now as opposed to "concentration" and "mental chatter." A very common pattern, especially during periods of intense awareness, is a flight to thought. In the work we are about to undertake, the words of Fritz Perls ring true: "Lose your mind and come to your senses."

In the way that we bring our awareness to the present, it is also important in the process of Archologie to bring our awareness to mythological transcendence, and, transgenerational resonance, thereby informing and revitalizing our existence from a source much deeper than itself. We will explore the ancestral and tribal influences on our lives as described by C.J.Jung, Bert Hellinger, and others.

WITNESSING: *Can I see myself clearly?*
As part of the process of Archologie, the simplest and most graphic definition of witnessing is to "become" a mirror reflecting any sensations or thoughts that arise without clinging to them or pushing them away, just as a mirror perfectly and impartially reflects whatever passes in front of it. Witnessing is the ability to step back and observe objectively what you are experiencing as a disinterested spectator while you are experiencing it.

In transcendent witnessing, you begin to treat all objects within the environment and indeed the environment itself as though they were part of you. Later in the book I will describe experiments that employ this method of mirroring, of becoming the room, the door, and so forth and noticing the sensations that arise.

LOYALTY: *Where have I come from?*

Family loyalty is the bond that holds the family together. We choose to stay loyal because we have received benefits and therefore we have a debt. The Webster definition of loyalty is: "a preferential commitment to a relationship based on indebtedness born of earned merit."

INTENTIONALITY: *Where am I going?*

Intentionality is the consciousness that converts sensory awareness into action in the external world, the environment. I sense it, I become aware of the sensation, I become energized, I mobilize myself, and I make contact with the environment. If the contact is complete, I am satisfied and I withdraw, and, my intent will have been complete. If it is not complete, with a strong ego I will try again, recognizing that the journey from sensation to withdrawal is life being lived.

SOUL: *The inner map*

The soul in the process of Archologie is the matrix upon which elements of our connections to our family, tribe and culture are imprinted. This imprint becomes our neuropsychological self: the self that creates our moral compass to navigate through the world.

Doors as a Metaphor

Many of the case studies and examples I introduce in this book revolve around the threshold and doorways. The doorway and it's components act as symbols or metaphors for the way we make our way through our lives. Doorways present opportunities…they act as barriers…and they are protectors. Doors create privacy, which is actually used for secrecy. Doorways welcome visitors or they keep them out; they are invitations or exclamations. The difference between the images is in our intent, not in the door being considered.

You might say that the front door is like the face, giving a first impression, indicating how accessible we are, and signaling to others what they might have to look forward to in the relationship. The doorknob is like a handshake. The handshake that tells us of trust and sincerity. And there is the threshold, sometimes referred to as the saddle, that requires us to step over it consciously both to enter and to depart. This conscious crossing over signals the transition from outer to inner and inner to outer and it conditions our behavior accordingly.

The back door is thought of as a secondary portal, used by immediate family, children, and those who deliver goods and services; it is a working door. Perhaps the back door is used for escape, a secret passage. Often, this door is neglected, like the parts of ourselves that we keep away from view, that we consider private and off limits to visitors. Both doors serve an important function.

My own ancestors came from an environment where the role of the door was critical in both the mundane and extraordinary aspects of life. The door kept out the cold and the animals, but ideally it would also keep out the Cosaks who came to drive them out of Poland. Of course, there are limits as to what you can ask a door to do.

The door being hinged is also a metaphor for our own style of selectivity, allowing some to enter and keeping others out.

Most doors are keyed and only a select few have the key; others must knock and ask for permission to enter. The door is a boundary that speaks eloquently about our needs in general and in specific. I may sleep with my bedroom door open, but I may choose to close it while making love. This may depend on external conditions such as the children being at home or internal ones not so easily named. The door intercedes on my behalf and says, "I will stand for you, open or closed, I am there for you." What a friend is the door.

I will use doorway as a metaphor for this process of Archologie, and self-discovery through relationship to our home space.

Exercise#1 The Doorway

A good way to begin this process of informed decision making is at your front door. Imagine that you are entering your home for the first time and you reach out to announce your arrival, what happens?

You grasp the doorknob, what happens?

You step over the threshold, what happens?

Be the door, speak as the door.

Is the door happy?

Is it feeling loved and attended to?

Does it feel like an important point of entry to your private world?

What is it saying right now?

Write it down, try not to sensor with your rational mind, just be a witness.

As a guide I offer the following sections to help you to "lose your mind and find your senses."

SECTION I- WHERE HAVE YOU COME FROM?

Chapter 1: Getting Started by Going Back

We start by going back and opening the doorway to the past. Experience the impact of your family-of-origin. Journey to the past through the use of the waking dream visualization.

Chapter 2: How Does Your Family-of-Origin Still Influence Your Choices?

When you step over the threshold of your front door, who else comes in with you? How does the culture of your family influence your space and the way that you inhabit it?

Chapter 3: How Does Your Childhood Continue to Influence You?

Recalling early childhood and its influence on your relationship to space. Play spaces that were encouraged and those that were not.

Chapter 4: Creating a Sense of Safety

Becoming the door

In the beginning where did I feel safe?

Chapter 5: "I Need My Space"

"I need my space" and other beliefs that come from the culture of the ancestors. The mythological door

Sorting out what is your inheritance and what you need now.

Chapter 6: My Personal Story of Connection to My Ancestors

Consciously crossing the threshold.

A brief memoir that explained so much to me.

Chapter 7: Uncovering the Family Tree

The hall with many doorways

A brief explanation of genograms, creating and using them to make connections.

Part 3: Intentional Living

The green door

Becoming aware of the changes in your consciousness.

Just when you think you can settle down and enjoy your life, new challenges arise, some from outer conditions and some from your inner being, perhaps as a reaction to outer conditions. Conditions like global warming, the cost of energy, and the desire to live a healthier productive life style have us all reassessing who we are, our relationship to the environment, and our homes.

As you begin this personal process journey, remember the only mistake you can make is not opening the door to look at all the spaces in your home and in your psyche. One space may hold the key for another and the reluctance to consider one may impede the opening of another. As you will see, the home can be used to fuel the reciprocity of life itself.

I have always had a "catch all" closet. I see this closet as a metaphor for my mind cluttered with random thoughts, ideas and issues that are bubbling away, longing to be sorted out to be useful and complete.

This closet may always be cluttered and that is OK, as long as I accept "what is". Ignoring the closet has psychic repercussions, that is, it is increasing the clutter. (A word of caution here- make sure the voice in the dialogue is yours and not someone else whose voice you have heard so often, you think it is yours). Hopefully dealing with it in this case means first having a dialogue with myself to see what needs to be done, and if this is the right moment to do it.

This is an extreme example but other metaphors like it can be found between your physical space and your inner psyche.

· · ·

Section One
Where Have You Come From?

Chapter 1:
Getting Started by Going Back

Archologie takes a step back from the practical to explore the roots in the positive and negative aspects of the past. We are tied to these aspects whether consciously or unconsciously, but in either case, they drive us. In addition to the influences of the past, there is our fantasy world, the one we invent but treat as real. Becoming informed of these states of being is the first step toward the choice of accepting or changing them.

How do we reflect the developed and undeveloped aspects of our family in our home? What traditions are honored, which are ignored and is there continuity between the generations?

We may not follow the ways of the past generations, but it is important to find ways to acknowledge those generations. In fact, the paradox is that if we do not acknowledge them, then our denial can lead to an unconscious following. Perhaps they lived in poverty and although we have sufficient money, we live as though we are impoverished. Perhaps they lived in a war-torn country and although we do not, we are in constant fear. There are hundreds of possible consequences.

Those who have a family tradition of maintaining an oral or written family history are fortunate. This tradition can provide a wealth of information that can sometimes explain events of the present as they unfold against the backdrop of the past. The stories can also be used as anecdotes, or they can be seen as a trans-generational resonance, holding clues to what is occurring now. In other words, there are repetitive patterns that occur in families long after the events that set them in motion. Some of these patterns are caused by genetics or environmental circumstances, such as famines or disease, or by attempts to show loyalty to a family through a way of being in the world.

The work of Bert Hellinger, a German philosopher, focuses on family loyalties and on the family dynamics where current events can be traced back to the past for their root cause. This may take the form, for example, of a current family member honoring an excluded family member through a distorted form of loyalty, which may include taking on characteristics such as illness or antisocial behavior that may have caused the original exclusion of that person from the family. The work of the biologist Ruppert Sheldrake is useful here to clarify the concept of trans-generational resonance. To paraphrase Sheldrake, we are each a hologram of our families, not just the DNA but also the character and values that constitute the family way. From this perspective, we can see how we might need to be conscious of the homes of our ancestors, since we may unconsciously be living in them anyway.

Exercise#2 Visualize a Journey to the Past

Visualization is a form of meditation. The primary difference is that visualization is like stepping into a time capsule and stepping out to another place. In the process, all doubts of arriving and being successful at experiencing what you came for are dismissed.

See yourself as an adult standing before your mother and father, behind them are their parents. Perhaps you can see one set of grandparents more clearly than the other, or a set of great grandparents may be visible as well. Ask your parents for their blessings for you to go back to visit the homeland of their parents (or grandparents, wherever your intuition tells you would be home).

See your parents part and allow you to pass through. You arrive at the home of your ancestors and knock at the door.

Your ancestors welcome you in and you stand at the threshold and look around at their home. Note what you see, smell, hear, the feeling of the floor as you remove your shoes and enter, the temperature of the air, the light, and what they offer you for sustenance.

You thank them for the visit. And they say you may take something from the house back with you to remember them.

What is it that you take?

You say goodbye, turn and come back to your parents, and you show them what you have brought back.

You note their reactions and you thank them for permitting you to visit the ancestors.

You return to the present.

While it is fresh in your mind, make note of your experience.

Be It Ever So Humble

Where did you go?

What did you experience when you knocked on the door, when the door was opened, when you stepped inside? Try to capture the details.

What was the source of light?

What was the source of heat?

What was the smell?

What were the sounds?

What was in the room?

How big was the room?

Who else was in the room?

And finally, what did you bring back?

Case Example: Flora takes this journey back and arrives at her grandfather's house. She sees herself on the landing of the stairs that also overlooks the dining room. She sees a large dining room table with her grandfather and his friends sitting around it. Flora hears them speaking, and feels the energy and excitement.

Coming back, she returns to her home in the present. She says she brought back the feeling of warmth and excitement she sensed from the people around the table, gathered by her grandfather.

In the present, Flora sees her own dining room where we are sitting, the smallest room in the house, with a cramped tiny table. She remarks that it lacks the qualities that she saw and was moved by her grandfather's house. We discussed what appeared in the past to be practical limitations to achieving a larger dining area. Now that a tangible image of what that dining room is has appeared, change is possible.

Case Example: Sally remembers the home of her maternal grandparents in Bangor County Cork, Ireland, which she visited as a child. Her visualization though is the home of her great grandparents. She enters and sees the home as uncluttered and elegant. It is filled with natural light. The floor is cool stone, cool grayish stone. The smell is clean and there is the aroma of fresh baking.

There is a bowl of lavender on the kitchen table. She says, "When I leave I take a little blue egg cup to bring back. I show the egg cup to my mother when I return, and tears of love fill her eyes, tears that say how much she felt for that place where she lived as a child. Her father looks sad and says, 'You never knew my home, the place where my parents lived.'"
Sally plans another visualization trip soon.

Case Example: Pete visualizes going back to his maternal grandparents on Long Island, over 100 years ago. He approaches the house, which is of wood, squarish in shape, and like all the others on the small street, it has a small porch. Pete says he is welcomed upon arrival and they sit on the porch, as it is hot and the dust from the road blows up toward the house when carriages pass. "It is very bright, the sun hurts my eyes," he says, and then continues, "My grandparents offer me a small cast iron skillet to take back; it is black. My grandmother says, 'This will be good when you have a home and prepare food for family and friends.' The skillet is heavy and cool, I know I will keep it with me always."

. . .

Chapter 2:
How Does Your Family-of-Origin Still Influence Your Choices?

Ironically, the awareness of the moment that I speak of throughout the book is deeply rooted in the ancestral and tribal past. It is widely recognized by cultural anthropologists that house form as well as site and street orientation among our ancestors was primarily influenced by mystical, symbolic and religious beliefs. Amos Rappoport, in his book *House Form and Culture* sites many examples including the Feng Shui system of China, where comfort must give way if it is at odds with the religious aspects.

It is easy to understand how strong these influences that can be seen as mystical, religious or tribal are when you see examples of how the forms and rules that evolved would be carried with the immigrants to the new lands that they settled in, even though they were inappropriate for the new place. As Rappoport says, "The symbolic character is important to them, however, it is a piece of *home*, and hence familiar in symbolic terms."

Whereas our ancestors had to consider the critical issue of physical restraints, weather, limited technology, as well as the mystical and religious symbolism mentioned above, today's choices are usually based on building codes, trends, and lender requirements. When there is personal choice, it is usually a decision to look forward or back. The novelty of the new or the familiarity of the old. This decision-making process can be exciting and begin to inform you of the ways of your ancestors. What were their attitudes, their "genre de vie" about the family coming together, privacy, the place of women in the home, the relationship of the home to the rest of the community, i.e., defining the threshold of privacy.

The home is thought of as a safe haven. It is the place in which under Anglo Saxon law, we are permitted to defend ourselves even to the extent of killing intruders in self-defense. Physical safety may be one of the primary reasons why we create our place, but there is a cultural diversity in the way safety and privacy are viewed. Usually, in very densely inhabited cultures, there was always a private domain outside the house in a courtyard, where the threshold of privacy was at the entry to the courtyard. This approach can be seen in India and the Middle East. In Anglo-European homes, the threshold would be in a garden behind a hedge.

In the United States, the threshold is at the front door, with an open lawn leading from the street, or a door opening directly into a public hall in the case of apartment homes.

Each of these solutions is a reflection of what Jung referred to as the collective unconscious. What we may not realize is that there may be a conflict when the current "collective" is at odds with the family culture. The right solution may not always be the easy or the obvious one. Let's use the issue of privacy in the home as an example. Privacy, like safety, has many definitions based on the cultural or tribal understanding of the individual in relationship to the [family] group and the greater community. The position of women in the culture will have an effect on the concept of privacy, especially where the women are protected from the view of outsiders. The need for privacy has created individual rooms and, in some cultures, separate dwellings for the same family. In other cultures, the individual can turn his or her back on the group and become "absent" and in effect invisible. In addition, attitudes toward sexuality and shame will determine the level of privacy needed to feel safe. This is another use of the word "safe," not the physical safety against intruders, but the psychological (mystical, religious) safety of the individual.

My personal experience of this "safety" comes from early childhood situations, which I will go into greater detail about in the next chapter. Some examples of the way I experience the impact as an adult is to feel more contained in a smaller space, with a warm usually incandescent light. When I am outdoors, feeling myself within a bounded area helps me feel safer; for example, a pool is preferable to a lake. As I write about these conditions for safety today, I am aware of how much I have changed in the last 20 years. *From my own experience I would suggest that there is a need to stop from time to time and reassess old beliefs and allow for changes and growth in yourself to be acknowledged. Here, I refer to the old tape that we play over and over until it is so worn that it hardly works any longer. We can stop the tape now.*

Paradoxically, this need for reassessment is paramount whether looking forward or back.

In looking back, I have found that the issues I had with family were inconsequential compared with what they contributed to the fabric of my life. In looking forward, I want to embrace them for who they are and what they have given me, but I also want to maintain my individuation. This feels like a healthy form of honoring, one my ancestors would approve of. I am certain of this, because I often heard them say that they wanted me to have it better than they did, a better education, a better life, in other words, like them and yet not like them. Even without the words we can imagine that their hardships are made worthwhile in part when we succeed, however we define that.

Case Example: Aaron and Sue and their daughter Emily live in a two-bedroom house. Aaron was raised in a home where there was no privacy. His parents had come from homes in Eastern Europe, where there was one large room for cooking, sleeping, and bathing. The desire for privacy was thought of as creating secrecy, and secrecy had negative connotations. As Emily became a teenager, she felt the need for more privacy to play her music, to call her friends and so forth, all part of a healthy individuation process. To achieve this privacy in the confines of a small house, Emily began to close her door. Aaron felt uncomfortable with Emily's growing independent attitude and the relationship with her peers that seemed such a strong influence. It was the closed door that created the conflict with Emily. It was the trigger that brought him to confront her. He went so far as threatening to remove the door. The closed door is the tangible evidence that made him aware of his inner feelings of the family loyalty being challenged. I asked Aaron to go through the following exercise with me, to see where clues might appear to help him better understand his rigid position with Emily about the closed door.

Exercise#3 What were my family's attitudes about the following

Privacy

The place of women in the home

The relationship of home to the extended community

Habits and customs of the family's coming together

Aaron's family understood that privacy was secrecy. His family believed that the woman should be protected and isolated from the community, relationships were set up by the parents, not the child. His family believed that home always remained central to the family members to the exclusion of all else. Peer influence was to be avoided. With these connections having been made, Aaron could share this with Emily and begin to change their tense relationship.

Case Example: Sally's paternal grandmother and her sister lived in the attic of her house when she was growing up, and Sally was not allowed in the attic, and neither was her mother. Sally's father liked his privacy and her brother had a great need for privacy. Sally had a rich inner life and was an avid reader.

Case Example: Pete grew up in a one-bathroom house. He recalls being in the bathtub with his older brother as kids when the teenage babysitter came in to urinate. "We covered up our pre-pubic loins demurely when Betty came in." As time went by and a new brother was on the way, my brother and I moved to the third floor and a separate bathroom was built, but by this time Pete's need for privacy was tempered by his early experience of sharing this usually private space.

The degree and style of privacy may be a clue to the feelings toward personal self-image, territoriality, and the place of the individual in the group, or it might be an indication of the socio-economic status of the family. As you look back at your family and tribe, all of the influences need to be evaluated in order to determine if there has been a slow-evolving change that you are building on, (being in connection) or is the change sudden and a rejection of the old ways (being out of connection). If the change represents rejection or is an effort to seek novelty for it's own sake, without an organic wholeness or an awareness that would allow for an acknowledgment of the ways of the ancestors, there could be a problem since *how* something is done may be more important than *what* is done.

. . .

Chapter 3:
How Does Your Childhood Continue to Influence You?

What is feeling safe for me? Safe is the space where I feel held, and protected, both physically and emotionally. Safe is the space where I can touch what I can see without fear. There is a sense of attachment that comes from the familiar, not necessarily from the objects within the space but from the space itself, the security, the regenerative quality and the creative quality as it begins to allow me to relax my limbic brain, reducing stress and need for fight or flight. In this relaxed state, the space that was small begins to expand and become the universe without walls or ceiling, but with a floor, or more accurately a foundation.

Reflecting on this process and going back to the earliest recollections of childhood has not been the easiest of tasks. There are moments when I am not certain which are remembered facts, which are stories, and which are idealized images.

As mentioned earlier, Jung said, "The work in progress becomes the Poet's fate and determines his psychic development. It is not Goethe that creates Faust, but Faust which creates Goethe." So it has been with me this last year as I have been writing this book. It has been the book that has, in a sense, created me and the feelings for family history that have arisen. The reflections on family both immediate and distant in time are shaping my thoughts and actions. I have experienced for myself the living proof of how loyalty, a word describing how I show my love and respect for family through the repetition of their patterns, and preferences, steers my course.

I would like to share some of these patterns as evidence, at least in my case, of how vulnerable we are to the influences of family. My first years were spent in a communal setting. The time was 1935, the tail end of the great depression. I was born into a small bungalow in Brighton beach, shared by parents with my grandmother and two of my mother's sisters. I was the first grandchild, and the first male born to this family. My image of this environment is close, warm, and golden in light. Necessity created this environment: the depression and newlyweds with little money, sharing with a parent, and helping with the rent. What I gain from this space, which is more than space, it is also a sensory container, is a sense of safety. It is my transition from the womb to the physical world. I emerge from the safety of an environment no larger than myself to the safe-nurturing closeness of others. The work of Robert Karen focuses on the attachments made during the first 18- to- 24 months of life, with a primary or substitute caretaker. My attachments to my grandmother and two aunts during that time felt very secure and I continue to search out other relationships to mirror those relationships. I believe I also identify the small crowded space with the good feelings. Good feelings in this case specifically refer to feeling safe, cared for, and therefore able to explore outwardly from a stable base.

My next home was a small apartment with my parents. They lived next door to my paternal grandparents. They were loving grandparents but I was the sixth grandchild and perhaps I was let down from a previous high of being the "only". I do not recall our apartment but I do have images of my grandparent's apartment, especially playing under their furniture, hiding or fortifying myself. I see the contrast of my physical appearance through photos. At ages 2 and 3, I was a robust happy child that at 6 and 7 turned pale and withdrawn. Was this shift due to the change in space and the lack of contact, starting school, feeling less special with paternal grandparents?

We moved again, this time to a two-bedroom apartment, where my sister was born. At age 10, I was dislocated from the room we shared and slept in the living room. This loss of privacy during these years of self-discovery made me seek out other venues, and the street and the vacant lots of Flatbush became very important to me. I felt a sense of darkness, danger, and aloneness. I learned about life, sex and the dark side through the detritus of the street. These were my secrets and the beginning of my secret life. Even today I find I enjoy being alone outdoors. I find it exciting and I am unbound, not relating to anyone else, but with a greater sense of creation.

At age 14, we purchased a row house, and I had my own bedroom. I had a choice of two rooms and I chose the smaller one, even though I was starting high school and my sister was seven years younger. The room is 7 feet by 10 feet and all of my life was in this room. Even through most of my college years I found safety in this small space, which contained a bed, dresser, desk and drawing table. When I reflect on this space I sense the urgency of keeping things that are important nearby and available for a quick departure. I am aware that this "readiness" is related to the program that uprooted my family during the mid-19th century in the Austro-Hungary of the Hapsburg Empire.

I spoke about the golden glow as I looked up from my first confined space. This memory was triggered by doing Exercise #1 in the first chapter. It is through that imaginal memory of that journey back in time and finding a safe space where I found elements from the past that I have kept alive. I can also recreate the sensual elements for myself, specifically the smells, sounds and touch of the past.

Smells are a particularly powerful trigger of childhood memories. I remember the aroma of cinnamon and raisins rolled in flat sheets of dough and then sliced and baked. This delicacy called Rugalach is still comfort food for me today seven decades later. I remember the underside of upholstered chairs and the stiff paper tags warning me: "Do not remove under penalty of law." These chairs were in the home of my paternal grandparents. I remember Tinker toys, Erector sets, and Lincoln logs (perhaps presaging my future as an architect), but not the specific space where I played with them. What is very clear and present are the street games played with other kids.

These games utilized the entirety of the environment around us: brick stoops, paved streets, curbs, corners, walls, even the cracks in the sidewalk and the small patches of dirt around street trees were a part of our daily play. The prize it turns out was to extend the home and it's safety into the neighborhood and the street, to expand the small two-bedroom apartment into a palace with the grounds of Versailles.

Having little recollection of my own play space, except for the lack of any place truly mine, I can wonder about the play space I created for my children.

For my two boys, who are three years apart in age, I built a play cube with a loft. This was their fortress, their imaginal safe haven from "the authorities". I asked them recently (now in their mid-40s) which were their favorite play spaces. They both indicated that their favorite places were outdoors. Since we lived in rural upstate New York, it was the dirt mounds and soft scape that got their attention along with their Tonka toys, miniature trucks and backhoes.

My daughter's play was very different, also in a rural setting, but in a house perhaps three times the size of the one I grew up in and twice the size of the home my sons did. In spite of its size, her play was the creation of small nests, some with just cushions, others with tents of blankets and still others under tables draped with cloth. I am making a conscious effort not to draw any conclusions from these experiences. I will leave it to you, the reader, to add your own experience and observations.

These observations may give you insights into what we as children seek out to fulfill our needs in order to grow into the adult who is at home in his or her environment, whatever it may be.

The childhoods I described just now span the years from 1935 through 1995, within which, time has allowed many dramatic changes, from space travel to plastics, and the solidification of television as a marketing tool without parallel, and the beginning of mass marketing and the "must have" syndrome.

But back to childhood play, where activities were in many ways creative and in many ways imitative of what adults were doing. There is an aspect of play inside and play outside that is worth looking at. That is the permeability of the home. As a child am I free to move in an out at will, or are there times to be in and times to be out that must be strictly adhered to? Is there a choice or is this a conditioned reaction to family traditions?

Case Example: Sally says, "In my home as a child, the two important rooms were the kitchen and the living room. When my mother's mother visited, she would be in the kitchen and would often cook. When my father's mother visited, on Sundays, she would sit in the living room. The kitchen was my mother's domain. It was large, warm and light with home-baked cookies in a jar on the window sill. My mother was always cooking, baking, washing, washing up. She was often there until late – 10 or 11 o'clock at night. She would seldom sit in the living room. I slept downstairs and if I was awake I would hear her noises from the kitchen: moving, working, clearing her throat, running the tap. Perhaps that was her privacy: her peace from the children who would sit in the living room, reading, playing cards or a game, sometimes fighting, and later on when we got a television, watching it. This was also where my father would play his music: classical, Ella Fitzgerald and Peggy Lee. It was a warm, busy, noisy room.

Case Example: Pete says, "I remember large family gatherings at Cooperstown. My aunts and uncle and a nephew and a niece would converge at Thanksgiving and at Christmas time, and my grandmother – a widow – and her older sister – a spinster – and their mother, my great-grandmother, would receive everybody. We would sit around a very large table in the kitchen in the daytime, and in the evening at a proper, long dining table in the dining room. Each family would occupy a guest room with its own bathroom, which otherwise would be let to visitors, of which there were many to the town. These occasions were loud, drink-filled evenings and more than once I can remember inebriated uncles erroneously making their way into my brother's and my bedroom on their way to bed. Women held forth: their voices were the loudest and longest into the evenings.

The kitchen was surrounded by a side porch, by an enormous back pantry (where my great grandmother would make fresh doughnuts!), by an adjacent room where chinaware and cutlery were kept, and by the dining room. Friends of the family would arrive by arrangement through the side porch and sit at the kitchen table. Very occasionally we would return their visits.

Case Example: Growing up in Eastern Prussia in the early 1950s Anna Maria would go out to play and have the door locked behind her. She could not come in until the door was opened again by one of her parents.

Case Example: Judith tells the story of growing up in Brooklyn in an apartment. Her parents would go outside and tell Judith she must stay inside. They did not know her fears about being alone in the house nor were they aware of her way of dealing with the fear. Judith would open the apartment door and place a chair right over the threshold with two legs in the house and two legs in the hall. Judith was hyper-vigilant against the intruder within and the intruder without.

Presumably, Anna Maria's and Judith's parents had rational reasons for their actions, perhaps peace in the house for a little while, or time to discuss important things privately, or control of "mess and dirt". However, the overarching feeling taken away by Anna Maria was, "My parents are not accessible." She vowed that she would always be sure to be accessible, especially to her children. In Judith's case, her early feeling of, "I must be hyper-vigilant and protect myself," led to a heightened perceptiveness, but also a guardedness that makes it difficult to let others in to share her personal space.

We can see in these examples where the home and the locked door have great significance to the youngster that is, first of all, feeling and second reasoning. Remember this example of the locked door when in Section II, Chapter 9 we look at the dialogue with inanimate objects like the front door. The door can speak, and we should not assume what it will say until it has spoken.

Exercise#3 Visualize your childhood play spaces, and any tastes and smells associated with them.

Chapter 4:
Creating a Sense of Safety

In the beginning, where did I feel safe? I felt safe in the small spaces, in the spaces that had warmth, and a sensuousness, comprised of many soft objects close at hand. I felt unsafe in the spaces that were larger and ordered, where keeping order was primary.

How does this feeling of safe space evolve? Why does it differ from person to person? After all, we are all carried the same way during pregnancy, and most of us are confined to small baby proof spaces for many months before we begin to cruise and explore. However, during the early stages, there may be significant differences in the way we are treated that may have an impact on the way we perceive and create space for ourselves in the future.

The field of neuroscience has been focusing on this aspect of early childhood development for the last ten years. Dr. Steve Porges of the University of Illinois at Chicago has published several papers describing how neural circuits in the limbic system, the old part of the brain, distinguish between what is safe and what is not. Porges has coined the term Neuroception to describe how these neural circuits function in the discernment process. A neuroception of safety is necessary before social engagement can begin. If I were to generalize about the criteria that create safe space, such as light, airy, and accessible to the exterior, I might not be describing the criteria for your safe space, which might include dimly lit, closed, and cloistered. To understand, accept and not judge these choices, especially in ourselves, is one aspect of this book. To see the origins of preferences and how they are patterned in early years is another. To make connections between what was and what is, and what can be seen and what is hidden, is the ultimate goal. To work with these connections rather than against them.

I will use my own case as an example of how my neuroception of safe space was created. I imagine beginning to explore the world in that small bungalow in Brighton Beach Brooklyn. I could get to all corners of that universe, I could cover a lot of ground one step at a time, and get lots of praise as well. As I ventured further out, I would turn and be assured that I was all right. As each new object came into reach, I gazed at it and turned back to see if I was O.K. This process of exploration and connectedness was the beginning of a secure attachment. As an adult, it is this experience that makes home the safest place, yet I still have the ability to explore and enjoy the unfamiliar, although with some reservations as you will see. The bungalow that was my grandmother's home was small, simple and all she could afford in 1900. I would guess it felt familiar to her having lived in the confines of a Shtetl in Eastern Europe until immigrating to America as a young adult, so that made it easier to accept (more about this in Chapter 6).

Unfortunately, this pleasant image is dimmed by the cloud of self-consciousness that passes over and casts it's shadow. In this world where privacy was at a premium, there was a prudishness, and I became self-conscious of my own and other's nakedness and struggled much of my youth with this uneasiness with nudity, which seemed to diminish the feeling of safety in this small communal home. I have heard that in the old world, privacy was created by turning the other way and becoming invisible, like in the child's game of hide-and-seek where children place their hands in front of their face and declare "You can't see me." It is two sides of the same and on the other side of safety is anxious protectiveness. Nakedness created a vulnerability for which I was not prepared for. The space was not in sync with the moral code, and the shame and vulnerability of nudity carried over into my outer relationships. In school I managed to get excused from swimming in order not to have to undress in public. The price I paid was not learning how to swim. How many other inhibitions did I acquire in growing up in that "safe" but "anxious" environment? In my case, the safety of the familiar environment had distinct boundaries that did not translate well to the greater environment. Perhaps this is the rule and not the exception, but the others with whom I grew up with had no fear of being naked. What did they get that I didn't? Was their safe space less anxious? Or did they have other inhibitions or "secret codes" I couldn't see?

As I think more about it, this cautious-safety extends like a net over all of my life: watch what you say, watch what you do, keep your assets liquid, and, most of all, do not draw attention to yourself. Occasionally, I have escaped the net: as an adolescent, buying my own bicycle; as a young adult, down-hill skiing, and later, driving a convertible. For me these were not trivial triumphs. They were my choices that would have never been considered by my father or imagined by my grandfather. What I achieved with these acts of free expression was to leave the anxieties where they belonged. Certain anxieties were not mine to carry; they belonged to others, some close by and some distant.

In addition to family loyalty where I felt the need to stay within the family's norm of behavior, there is a desire to protect my parents. It has been seen again and again that a child will sacrifice him or herself to save the parent or the parental relationship. If there is a hole (something missing in the family system) a child will take on a role that will fill the hole. This process can rob the child of a sense of their true self, and the process of rediscovering that self can be long and arduous, but no question, worth the effort. Al Pesso a psychotherapist in Franklin, New Hampshire, does group therapy around "Holes and Roles," offering a way back to the self by seeing that the hole we may have filled was created by a piece missing in the childhood of our parents or their parents.

In recognizing the loyalties and roles that we assume early in life, we are more free to begin to explore a more authentic way of being. For some it will be small steps like deciding to have a television in the bedroom, or not to eat dinner in the kitchen. In order to discern the relevance or rightness of these decisions for you in this moment, they must be examined by exploring the inner voices that are directing you. Allow yourself to have a dialogue with these voices, let them know that you are letting go of the role you have been carrying for so long, and leaving it outside the front door of your home.

Where are you in this process of finding your authentic self? Is the "real you" in hiding? Can you put down the baggage of your ancestors and say to them, "Thank you for taking me on this journey, I appreciate all I have been given, but these anxieties are not mine and I leave them here with you as I continue to grow. I will continue to honor you and keep you in my heart and my home."

The noted Author and Professor of Architecture, Witold Rybczynski, in his book *Home - A Short History of an Idea* writes about comfort (perhaps another way of describing safety): "Understanding comfort is like trying to describe an onion. It appears simple on the outside, just a sphere in shape. But this is deceptive, for an onion also has many layers. If we cut it apart, we are left with a pile of onion skins, but the original form has disappeared; if we describe each layer separately, we lose sight of the whole. To complicate matters further, the layers are transparent, so that when we look at the whole onion we see not just the surface but also something of the interior. Similarly comfort (safety) is both something simple and complicated. It incorporates many transparent layers of meaning- privacy, ease, convenience, some of which are buried deeper than others." Rybczynski tells us that comfort and safety involve a combination of sensations, many of them subconscious, and in his final bit of advice he offers: "We should resist the inadequate definitions that engineers and architects have offered us. Domestic well being is too important to be left to the experts; it is as it has always been, the business of the family and the individual."

> ## Exercise#4 What are your memories of situations in which you felt safe and situations in which you felt anxious in early childhood?

Remember that memory is not reliable, especially up to three years of age, and so it may be the stories surrounding the circumstances that you recall.

Who was the primary caretaker?

Where was the caretaking done? Was there more than one person or place?

Was there a set pattern to the caretaking?

List your responses without analyzing or setting meaning to the answers. Sit with the exercise theme a while before responding to the specific questions being posed.

Case Example: Sally notes, "I am most comfortable at home when the house is warm enough so I can have bare arms. I like the place to be light in the sense of airy, not in the sense of bright lighting. I prefer light or neutral colors on walls, ceilings and floors. Where I live in Manchester, England, there are often grey skies, and I need varying types of illumination to help it feel bright inside when it is gloomy outside. I enjoy cooking smells, as well as the smell of a clean fresh home."

Case Example: Pete (who lives with Sally in Manchester) says, "I like fresh air, good ventilation. I need bright light to read, but indirect light otherwise. I love the smell of cooking in the kitchen, but not upstairs in the bedrooms afterwards. Strong smells of garlic, roasting meat, and baking are for me all warming, connecting sensations, a kind of sensuousness going through my blood and around my body. I am conflicted when it comes to skin temperature between turning the heat to warm allowing for a tee-shirt and sandals, and covering up to adjust to the natural temperature."

Exercise#4A Get in touch with your neural circuits, become aware of your patterns of safety

What is the skin temperature at which you feel safe?

What are the smells that make you feel safe?

What smells can you tolerate some of the time?

What smells can you not tolerate at all?

Chapter 5:
"I Need My Space"

My first adult home, designed and built by me for my wife and two boys, was focused on economy, and environmental sustainability (in 1965). It was an open plan house, perhaps echoing the shtetl life, where privacy had to be consciously arranged or was more a state of mind than a state of being.

Ten years later, after a separation and divorce, the nuclear family sold the house and moved into a communal setting, where we each had our own room and once again I found myself in the room of my early teens. Once again all my worldly possessions were close by and ready to be gathered up on a moment's notice.

Once again there was a sense of the container being the space and the closeness that was created, felt supportive.

The image of a spiral comes up in my mind here where events seem to recur but perhaps on a deeper level (depending on how conscious we make ourselves of them) in order to resolve or at least to recognize their significance to our evolutionary being.

Some decisions we make in creating our home spaces might carry the quality and feeling of the ancestral space and others will appear to reject aspects that are no longer practical or relevant. In many cases a condition that was created by scarcity or deprivation became the familiar and safe situation. Our ancestors survived by creating these safe places, and our debt to them is often repaid by unconsciously recreating them in our current environments. Often when we ignore the tribal influences, there is a price to pay. This is not to say that we must follow the old forms, but rather that we must acknowledge them and the way in which they created safety and supported survival. For one thing, without them, you and I would not be here.

It took seven years more to find the space I am now in with my second wife. Marrying Alexis and having a child together took us to the suburbs where Alexis found the house of her dreams, and I helped facilitate its purchase. The house has large open rooms, each with views of gardens and long vistas down a meadow. Realizing that I am happily here is a testament to my willingness to share and care for another, but I am also aware that I did not create "my space" until the writing of this book when it became necessary to allow the space, physically and mentally for its completion. I also have to allow for the possibility that I have experienced a paradigm shift and I no longer fear for my existence in this open space. Perhaps I can say to my ancestors, "I understand why you were always prepared to move on, and I honor you by now declaring my right and choice to stay. Thank you for giving me the opportunity to show you this new part of me, that comes from a deep and heartfelt part of me that will always be connected to you."

If you can become fully aware of your needs in order to create comfort, you will not have to look to others to tell you what these needs are. This awareness will make it possible to take responsibility for your own actions, not living for the moment, which is defined as hedonism, but rather living in the moment.

Case Example: Sally reveals, "I honor my maternal ancestors around our table with the color blue, and the Spode Italian chinaware in our kitchen. In that kitchen, there is the rocking chair that belonged to my maternal grandmother, which I rocked in with her as a little girl."

Case Example: Pete articulates, "Until recently I did not honor my ancestors, especially on my father's side. I am making efforts to learn more about this side of the family. I am not sure yet what form this change in me will take in my home. Photographs do not do it for me. I have many documents from my mother's keepsakes as does my brother. We have spoken about doing something with these documents to honor the ancestors."

Exercise#5

What are the Family /Tribal influences that influence your lifestyle?

Do you think there has been a price to pay for holding on to these influences?

Are there influences that you know you have let go of? Is there so-called "baggage" you carry for others?

Do you think there will be a price to pay for letting go of those influences?

> ## Exercise#5A Forms of honoring the ancestors. Has it ever occurred to you that honoring the ancestors may have relevance in your current life?

How do you currently honor your ancestors?

Where do you honor the ancestors (family tree or genogram, photo wall, valued objects or furnishings)?

Have you intended to honor your ancestors but not acted on it?

What feelings arise in you if you answered affirmatively to the previous question?

Whatever form the honoring of ancestors takes, creating a conscious acknowledgment is an important part of the process of finding your real self and allowing the expression of that self to be reflected in your home. This reciprocity is energizing and life-affirming.

Chapter 6:
My Personal Story of Connection
to My Ancestors

My grandmother spoke no English. As my primary caretaker, since my mother and father needed to work, she spoke to me and, more significantly, sang to me in Yiddish. She baked and cooked and sewed. I remember the times in that small cottage in Brighton Beach Brooklyn. Crowded was not a description that fit, it was shared space that was a way of life that colored my approach to personal space. I was in that environment until about three years old, so my need for privacy was not yet discovered. What I did find was the magic of fantasy and creative self-play. I have been kidded about what appears to be my preference for small, dark and uncluttered (this last criterion is a modification) space where sensations, not objects, and connections, not things, are paramount.

I would like to think that this observation to the extent it is true comes from this early experience. I would also like to believe that there are influences from old traditions, tribal ways of entering the world and becoming part of it. The question arises in me: what would have happened if my grandmother and my mother's sisters were not around? My mother's way would have been the only way I would have known, both in her style of attachment and in the style that she created "home." Her style was to make sure everything was in place, even to the extent that it appeared unlived in. Life had to be reliable, which meant sameness from one day to the next.

I now see this style as a response on her part to three things. The first was the uncertainty and hardship experienced by her parents as they left their native land to immigrate to the new world. The second was the traumatic loss of her father when she was 12 years old; the oldest of six, with a mother who spoke no English and could not support her family. The third was the need for her to assimilate to her adopted culture; in her mind perhaps that meant turning her back on the "old world." One way to do that was to create a home where objects and the overall image became more important than the sensations or connections of the family dwelling there. This seems like such a natural and even healthy way to be, a way of moving on and individuating. However I now know that there is a price: the sense of wholeness that comes from honoring the past generations is given up in the exchange.

In this black and white container, the portions that are rejected must be cut away, must be forgotten, in order to embrace the new without feeling guilt or grief.

In this movement, the container of culture or family is not valued. In the black-and-white container model there is upward mobilization, with no awareness of regret, sadness, longing, or mourning. This is often a pitfall in the process of assimilation.

It has taken me many years and much personal reflection to become aware and then to acknowledge that I feel sadness and loss at not having a sense of the continuity with the past generations. Being unconscious of that need as a child of the 1940s and 1950s, I did not ask the right questions or get the oral history so that I could pass that on to my children.

I have researched and written a history as far back as the generation of my grandparents. I have also done a genogram of my family (see chapter 7 for guidance on how to do this). This graphic representation of the generations and the interconnections or avoidances of the family members is an invaluable tool to understanding the family culture. Where I have not had access to factual history, I have attempted to contact the past in dreams (see chapter 8) and with guided imagery.

On the surface there appears to be a big difference between dreams and guided imagery. Dreams come in deep sleep and can be repetitious wanderings through unfamiliar landscapes. Sometimes the dream is treated as a metaphor, and some believe that dreams are a co-creation between the conscious and unconscious self. This description of a dream fits with the description of guided imagery. Images are suggested, they rise and fall away, leading us to the place we need to go to find a missing part of our self. We are led by what is familiar. The images come to us and we create them at the same time. We are the writer, director, and actor.

Exercise#6 Tell your personal story

One of the reasons for sharing parts of my own childhood story is so you can begin making connections between knowledge about your past and gaps in that knowledge and how that past informs how you live in the present. It is an opportunity to explore what you know and what stands out as meaningful (without judgment) and maybe even what you don't know but have a suspicion might be helpful. Take this opportunity to write down your personal story. Do not dwell on judgments or interpretations but rather just the facts, the people, the time, and the place. Once this is laid out, you may begin to find bridges between what was and what is now.

Chapter 7:
Uncovering the Family Tree

I think my story is a common one where parents are struggling to provide a home for themselves and their children, and may choose to look away from their ancestral origins in order to create something of their own. In doing so there may be an unintentional rejection of the old ways, and as the pendulum swings there may be a need to find the balance. That balance may be provided now by acknowledging that the ancestors' presence in our lives is part of the personal growth process, the process of maturing and seeing the whole tree from the nurturing roots to the newest sprouting buds.

The creation of the family tree or genogram begins with asking questions of the elders; such questions will help establish the country or region of origin, living style (itinerant, landed farming, urban intellectual, etc.) and other variables that make up a life profile. Where there are no longer any elders, internet research or turning to old letters or journals may support your journey back.

Ask questions that go beyond the well-marked and acknowledged events. This information may reveal some things about the family style of communication and levels of privacy or communal sharing; for example, a sentence like this can be very rich in overt and covert information: "While Mother was hospitalized after your birth, Aunt Molly took care of you for the first 18 months of your life." Find out more about Molly. Where was she living? With whom? What was the house like? Are there any pictures available?

Your need to know and to honor may allow for an important story to be told, which will benefit you and those who come later.

I have included the genogram of my family here as an example. For more information on genograms I recommend the work of Monica McGoldrick.

The Kerner / Levinson Genogram

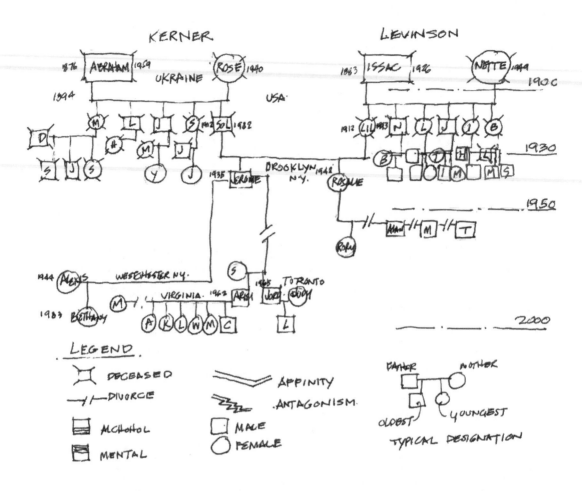

There is no one left who can fill in more of those who came earlier. Sadly, my thirst for this knowledge comes too late and yet even my interest is a way of honoring those who came before.

Exercise#7 Create your family's genogram

Chapter 8:
Dreams

Dreams are another form of threshold: that transition from awakeness, where the mind and the senses are both guiding and reacting to the activities and stimuli of the day, to the half sleep and sleep of waking dreams and deep dreaming. Dreaming in these states seems to bring forth images from a deep reservoir of memories and anticipations. These images can be useful if observed from a detached neutral position, as if observing someone else's painting in a gallery. From Carl Jung's perspective on dreams, we learn that a tool for interpreting the dream is to meet every part and aspect of the dream, and be in dialogue with each part. In Fritz Perls' Gestalt therapy practice you would become each aspect or part of the dream. In both approaches, the dialogue is a key to finding meaning.

Imagine your dream takes you through long hallways to a rooftop and the only way down is to scale a wall and then leap to the roof below. From there, you must jump into the water where there is a small boat waiting to take you to an island. In the Gestalt model, you first see the images as a picture and then you become each part of the picture. As that part, you speak the word or words that describe your role. Write down the key elements of the dream upon waking, or in the case of the waking dream or day-dreaming, as soon as you come to the present. As with many experiences in life, the significance of these dreams may take some time to become clear. Sitting with the lack of clarity and the confusion is an important step in the process.

In the dream described next, I made contact with feelings about my paternal grandfather. These feelings became building blocks for further discovery about my ancestors, and each discovery of feeling and fact helped me get over the threshold into my home. The home is both my soul and my soul's longing to enter a room and see and know my true self.

In my dream I am lying on a beach and see the balloons that I had let go of. The balloons are caught in the treetops, their colors are fading but they are not deflating. This image haunts me, as though I missed his humanity as a child growing up and let go of him, as if he were one of the balloons. I missed him in later years.

I did not grieve for him when he died. He was the old man I never knew. I let go of him and then I let go of the sadness of both not knowing him and then of losing him.

Reconnecting with Abraham through this dream and stirring up those lost feelings has made my life richer. The dream is a prelude to the dialogue with Abraham in Chapter 9. It is the subconscious connection that I made with Abraham that made me aware that he would be the ancestor with whom I would begin to have the dialogue, the one with whom I wanted to share and from whom I wanted to gain approval. My next step would be to ask for a dream where Abraham would guide me back to the space where he grew up, where he felt safe.

In the next exercise I will ask you to record your dreams for two weeks. Since we are interested in the areas of home and family I ask that you focus your thoughts and energy on those aspects. Set the stage for dreams by asking a question and writing it down before going to bed, such as; where did I enjoy playing as a child? Or, is there an ancestor whom I need to meet?

I have been helped to dream both in sleep and through guided visualization by the teaching of Judith Schmidt PhD and the program she and Alexis Johnson PhD have created through The Center for Intentional Living. Dr. Schmidt continues the lineage of Collette, a noted Dream therapist and poet who lives and works in Jerusalem. A good source book for dreaming, which serves as a solid introduction to creative and evocative dreaming, is Rachael Bratnick's *Awakening the Dreamer.*

> # Exercise#8 Record your dreams about family and home for two weeks.

You may ask for specific requests, but because dreams can be obscure and indirect, all dreams should be noted.

Section Two
Where are You Now?

Chapter 9:
Becoming a Witness for Yourself

We have come a long way in the last 500 years in terms of how we create shelter, with most of the innovations contributing to comfort occurring in the last 100 years. Where there were once small openings in order to keep out the cold or heat or predators, we now have the ability to use insulated glass enclosing conditioned space and conquer darkness with artificial light.

These technological advances can mask but they cannot change our origins and their influence on our psyche. Our souls are imprinted with the past and the ways in which our ancestors made the path for us. We may not choose to follow that path, but we benefit when we acknowledge it and honor it, and so do our children and theirs.

As discussed in Chapter 1, among the dramatic changes that have occurred in my lifetime are growth of powerful mass marketing and "the must have" syndrome that has resulted. As young children, we are told what play thing is essential to have; as adolescents, we are bombarded with "must-have" electronic gadgets; and as adults, we are seduced by "must-have" kitchens or baths. The values, mythology and patterns of family, tribe, and, culture have given way to national and global values, mythologies and patterns. We live in a global society where news is transmitted instantly, and we feel the pull to bring our attention to many directions simultaneously. From this place it is difficult to connect with our inner core, to stay connected to the source of our life as well as the sources of our sustenance. The evidence is all around us.

There is a sense of rootlessness in our society. Statistics show that the average duration for a family to remain in one home is five years. Self-medication of all kinds is rampant among all strata of the population, relationships are disposable, and people are searching for ways to feel grounded in a fast-moving global culture. The reasons are too many to explore here but we are all touched by this rootlessness.

One way to meet the challenge is by establishing a home base in connection with roots, with a sense of coming from somewhere, a life force already in place that can serve as a wellspring for well being. Clearly the presence of parents and their involvement with children will do much to uphold the family's values, and some might argue that family history moves with the family, but the inclusion of family must be done with consciousness and diligence.

There is some irony in the current situation that we face due to our dependence on fossil fuels in order to maintain our comfort and lifestyles. We are hearing the words "sustainability" and "green" every day now. Perhaps there is more to be gained from a look back at our ancestors and the way they touched the earth and used it's resources. I will say more about this in Section III on intentionality.

There are many forms of honoring: a family photo wall, a piece of furniture belonging to grandparents, setting the table for a holiday feast the way mom did, and more. A more active form of honoring might be a dialogue with the ancestors to seek council, or to satisfy our curiosity as to how they feel in the spaces we call home.

Is there a break in the generations? Is it possible to have a dialogue with those souls who have departed so long ago? There is little to lose in trying (except your skepticism) and there is much to gain.

Why is it important to hear these voices? In order to verbalize and expose what is in the background anyway. You may hear praise or perhaps shaming for being disloyal to the family way. The critical voice that speaks of disloyalty is what I refer to as the baggage in the sense that there are many ways to express loyalty to the family without repeating lifestyles that are no longer applicable. If you can put down the baggage and say to the ancestors: "I thank you for carrying this, it was important to you, and it enabled the family to be where it is today, but I no longer need this in my life," you stake your claim to your reality without rejecting them. This shift can allow you to begin to make decisions based on your needs and not the need to keep peace with the ancestors. So much of our frustration and dissatisfaction with where we live is based on a discontinuity between the seen and unseen aspects of ancestral connection. Bring the unconscious dialogue to the surface, which can call the secret discord so that the ancestors have a way to be in your life, a part of it in a good way rather than in a conflictual way.

Exercise#9 Moving Through Time and Space

As you move through your space allow older generations to express how they feel about the space. This process, based on Gestalt experiments (see Joseph Zinker, *Creative Process in Gestalt Therapy*) is usually done with an empty chair across from you. The person you bring in to sit on the empty chair speaks through you as you sit in their chair, then you return to your chair to respond, observing how you feel in the space in between, the so-called " meta space" where you can observe yourself and your reactions, without judging them. Here is a portion of the imaginary dialogue with my Grandfather Abraham, as I show him around my home;

Example: Jerome and Grandfather Abraham
Abraham: "Why so much glass? You will freeze your tuchas," and then, "Why so much heat, if you are cold then put on a sweater." There is a simple wisdom in these admonishments: I have a sense of shame for being impractical and wasteful. I try to explain.
Jerome: "I am too busy to heat with wood or coal, collecting the wood and tending the fire is too time-consuming, but I do what I can to conserve energy." He listens with understanding, but responds with more questions.
Abraham: "Why are the rooms so big? Why are the window openings so bare?"
Jerome: "We enjoy having our friends in and entertaining them, and we love the unobstructed view from each of the windows."
From his point of view, his questions have nothing to do with the environment and certainly not global warming. They reflect the direct experience of one who had few options and where the most cost-effective methods had to prevail.
We continue our dialogue.
Jerome: "There is no going back to your day where there were many fewer people and fewer needs for energy in a world that had no electronics or automation."
Abraham: "I see these as improvements, but maybe you have gone too far from what is reasonable, from a healthy balance in your life."
Jerome: "Are you being self-righteous? You smoke and are overweight. Aren't I in better health than when you were the age I am now. Your son (my father) never made it to my age."
He shakes his head as if to concede this point.
I feel the dialogue straying into areas far from this chapter, so I bring it back with a question.
Jerome: "How was it for you growing up in the shtetl?"

Be It Ever So Humble

Abraham: "My memory is not all that clear but what I do recall is a closeness and sharing, both of the fruit of the land and of the labor to obtain it."

He describes the home as I had imagined it (perhaps we had spoken before) in a dream or a visualization exercise.

> ## Exercise#10 Have a dialogue about your home with an ancestor.

Standing at the front door, see whom you are with, say the name(s) out loud and tell the person how you are feeling right now as you are opening the door to show him or her in.

As you step over the threshold, ask how it feels to enter your home.

Walk to each room and ask a question, one that seems to emerge organically. What do you see that you like in here? What do you think of the light, the sounds?

Between each question, leave room for a response, and taking a step to the right or left, allow the ancestor's voice to come through.

This imaginary journey may inform you about some of your own hidden feelings about your home, but you need to tune into whether these feelings are authentic to you or are your way of remaining loyal to the ancestors. If a feeling emerges in you during the walk through, ask the ancestor how he or she feels about it: betrayal, lack of loyalty, disregard? Perhaps this person feels proud of how you have come to this new place and wishes to be remembered in some small way that you create, rather than honored through imitation.

After you have had the experience of the dialogue with an ancestor and seen it through his or her eyes, you are now ready to begin your own journey into your home. Before you do, I want to take a moment and return to the concept of a witness. As I define "witnessing," it is the ability to step back and observe objectively what you are experiencing as a disinterested spectator, while you are experiencing it. A primary goal is to objectively see yourself in your home as others see you, without judgment.

In the spirit of transcendent unity (see Ken Wilbur, *No Boundary*) you will become the other object and/or space and allow that object to speak through you. Do not sensor or filter the words. After each "conversation," you may want to note significant discoveries. What might you discover during this exercise? The front door may feel underutilized, not cared for, second to the back door, useless, irrelevant.

You may respond as your rational self, with all the practical reasons, but be sure to hear the door, see where there is a part of you that may have a similar longing or feeling.

Perhaps a more welcoming attitude toward friends or extended family, without sacrificing your privacy and family intimacy, is the message. Perhaps there is something else that has remained unspoken for too long.

The entry hall is next. Or perhaps it is the lack of one. Is there a place of arrival into your home, a place to put down a package or remove wet shoes? In this dialogue, there may be several variations: for example, imagine who might be entering the house. Is it your best friend, your mother-in-law, the cable guy?

The more specific you can be as you imagine these people entering your home, the more information will become available to you as to how you feel towards the space and about your self within the space.

I will ask you to follow this procedure through each room - kitchen, bathroom, bedroom and so on – later in Chapter 12.

The author with Grandfather Abraham at graduation from Pratt Institute 1958

Exercise #11 Dialogue Between Self and Inanimate Objects

Note: This is a repeat of exercise #1, do not skip it!

(This exercise is best done alone.) Starting at the front door, begin by having a dialogue with the door. Place two pieces of paper on the floor in front of the door. One paper will represent the door (object or space), and the other paper, will represent you. The space in between, the meta space, is the neutral zone as you travel in the middle of the two.

I will offer an example here as a demonstration of the process in the form of an enactment.

Case Example: Sally and Pete asked me to consult on their plan to redo the ground floor of their townhouse. Their goal was to renovate the kitchen and dining room, relocating the kitchen so it would be between the living room and the dining room, which placed it in full view of the entry hall.

I set the stage for them: it is a rainy Saturday night and two other couples are coming over for a dinner party. I ask Sally to take it from there, being very specific, that is, giving names to the guests, and beginning with the doorbell ringing. She describes the doorbell ringing and Pete going to the door to let the guests in. She describes the raincoats and umbrellas being shed, while she makes last-minute preparations in the kitchen. At this point, I notice Sally tense up, her facial expression changing, and stress lines appearing around her eyes and mouth. I asked her to tell me what is going on, what thoughts she is having. She replies, "I feel anxious, I am not ready, the kitchen is a mess and our company has arrived." What Sally was telling me is that she did not feel safe. The new location of the kitchen was a preconceived idea (versus one internally inspired), perhaps taken from the pages of a kitchen design book, but it did not reflect the level of safety required by Sally. With this new information in mind, I created an alternate sketch, with the kitchen off to the side, where the dining room was. Sally could feel the difference immediately. I then created a seating area as part of the new dining room that would be visible from the kitchen, so that Sally would not feel isolated in the event she had not yet finished with preparations for dinner when the guests were arriving.

My attention to her stress level and the expression of it in her body and on her face told me that something was wrong. Observing the whole person including the non-verbal cues, is critical to getting a complete picture. Can you do this for yourself? Can you be a mirror noting your reactions to objects or space as you walk through your home, without censorship? It might be difficult, but it is possible. Keep in mind that the difficulty may be in your desire to have the "idealized solution" rather than the comfortable one, reflecting your personal preference. This conflict of interest might be compared to someone choosing to wear a trendy shoe but suffering the discomfort (and blister) to do so.

Illustration- Sally and Pete's floor plan: Original and Revised.

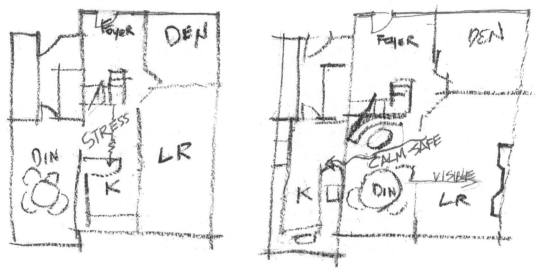

Original Plan   **Revised Plan**

Although the previous example was created on paper, the same can be done in the actual space. Remember, you are taking an inventory, listening to the space, and the objects, and noting your own reactions, which may also incorporate the other voices including judgments or praise, real or imagined. As all of these voices are heard and you feel they are important, stop and dialogue with the source. Use the chair experiment discussed earlier to hear the point of view being expressed by those voices and respond with yours. This is not an argument; it is sweeping out the corners of the mind and allowing for a fresh approach. Keep a journal of the dialogues and see what emerges as time goes by.

What anxieties are you holding, and how are they reflected in your home? Have they grown larger than life in the dark? What does this monster look like?

In Section II, Chapter 10, I will ask you to look at and express these anxieties, concerns, and disappointments in the Reality plan. There is a lot of creative energy locked away in the aspect of yourself that is judgmental and critical of your space. The second exercise will ask you to express your thoughts and images of fantasies, those spaces that are or perhaps have been forbidden in the past, but are very much alive in your subconscious. If we can unleash the energy being held in the anxious reality and the fantasy, a wave of creativity will follow and may surprise you. The fear may be how to afford it or how to settle for anything less. These are better issues to deal with than being frozen and dissatisfied. Once the door is open to new energy and creativity, obstacles truly do become opportunities.

Residence with tower, South Salem, NY, designed by the author

• • •

Chapter 10:
The Reality and the Ideal Plans

Before the "Ideal," there is the reality plan. In some cases, reality, which is your acknowledgment of "what is," may exaggerate negative or undeveloped aspects of your space, or understate the positive or developed aspects. The way that you exaggerate the circumstance may be your own or it may be the family style that I refer to as baggage. In either case, you need to go there before you can create a fantasy of how things might change.

There is often anxiety around the reality plan. This plan can be judgmental and unforgiving. Allow yourself this liberty; this is where you can place the blame on external circumstances. This is the time when you can vent your annoyance at conditions that you consider beyond your control and that seem to create your reality.

I would like to reiterate some of the experiments that will assist you in getting in touch with these feelings about developed or undeveloped aspects of your home. I use the terms developed and undeveloped rather than negative or positive to avoid labeling them as good or bad. They are neither good nor bad: they are what they are, a reflection of your current state.

Allow yourself the latitude to express the broadest spectrum of feelings you can connect with. These may include some of the seven deadly sins, such as greed and envy. You will find that expressing them will energize you. The ideal may lie at the other end of the spectrum. It is the plan that you might create if there were no obstacles such as time or money, or other external influences dictating a solution. Here too we can see the family loyalty appear: perhaps the historical family feels it is idle foolishness to fantasize, even blasphemous to do so, or perhaps there is something sinful or ungracious in focusing on the negative in working with the reality plan.

In either case, you need to see where this attitude on your part comes from, but more important to determine if it deters you from doing this exercise. You can see from this perspective how important it is to connect with the culture of the family and the family culture; that is, with it's values, preferences, and prejudices, as you proceed to create your living environment. This activity is akin to the potter who must understand the nature of the clay, it's content and characteristics, before throwing a pot.

So it is with yourself needing to find your limits, preferences and prejudices. If they are the same as those of the family, then are you in sync with them today. Or are you holding those same limits, preferences and prejudices out of loyalty. If they are not the family's, ask yourself the question: "Have I rejected the family values in order to individuate, and have I accomplished that goal without guilt and a fear of dishonoring them? Is this process of acceptance and rejection of family values like a pendulum swinging between the extremes of acceptance and rejection, where the poles seem easier to accept until a balance point can be found?

Exercise#12 Unfinished Family Business

Have an imaginal dialogue with your family of origin. This dialogue consists of an inventory of unfinished business between you and them and your ancestors. Allow space for their reactions. Do not respond but note your own reactions and move on. The goal of this exercise is not to change the family but to make a decision to leave the baggage outside the front door as you continue the process of discovery. You can open the door and revisit any of the issues, at any time, when you are ready. Here are some sample issues for your dialogue. Making the issues your own is important.

Mama, why didn't you take baths and teach me how to as well?

Papa, how come you never would allow music to be played in the house?

Why were the doors always kept open?

Why were the curtains always kept drawn?

Why did you never speak about your homeland?

Case Example: Matt and Karen were trying to have a child, and they were experiencing difficulty. They lived in a spacious apartment in a brownstone. I asked them to make a drawing of the apartment from memory as we sat at the kitchen table. They did the drawing together. When the drawing was complete, it was apparent that there was no space left on the paper, for the room that would be dedicated to the future nursery. This graphic Rorschach was an "out picturing" of one of their issues around conceiving.

I asked them each to go back to Chapter 2 and look at their own childhoods and see where it may be still influencing them today. Matt spoke about his parents, who were Holocaust survivors, being anxious and fearful as they raised him in this new country. Their anxiety and difficulty in making ends meet left a scar that Matt still has today. He fears that he does not have the emotional or financial strength to support a child, to create a safe environment, a physical container for the child. By sharing this image and challenging the reality of it, change is possible. Matt was able to see that the baggage he had been carrying does not belong to him but rather to his father. Matt was able to put that piece of baggage down, and, bowing to his father, acknowledge his father's struggle and also his own gratitude to his father for all he was able to provide the family. Although Karen participated in the exercise, the key issue belonged with Matt. Karen was able then to reinforce the reality of her husband's ability to support the family they had envisioned.

Case Example: Mary and Tom were married 13 years with three children, 10, 7, and 4. They lived in a large, recently built house with signs of the children everywhere. Mary had no place of refuge (safe space); even the bedroom had been taken over as a golf practice area, with a tee and threeway mirror at the foot of the bed. Tom's inner child had taken over that space.

Was the underlying problem of Mary's feeling of having no "refuge" the lack of boundaries of the children and the dad? Was this the outcome of a style of attachment that had been passed on from prior generations, where freedom without restrictions is substituted for secure attachment that allows for discipline? The key in this case was out-pictured in the bedroom.

There are several approaches that could be taken to examine the dynamics that are having an impact on the home. One would be to bring the ancestors into the bedroom and ask them what they see there and ask their advice if they see a problem. A second approach might be to see the bedroom as a dream and to ask Mary and Tom to each speak as part of the dream and compare their imagery. A third approach might be to have Mary and Tom each have a dialogue with both the bed and the golf practice tee. I chose the latter approach and asked Tom to begin.

Tom to the bed: "Why do you have to hog so much space, we only sleep here."

Tom as the bed: "I don't mind your golf activities, they don't prevent me from doing my job."

Mary to the bed: "I used to look forward to snuggling under the covers and feeling close to Tom, lately you feel like part of the locker room."

Mary as the bed: "I miss that too; those were intimate times that meant a lot after a long day alone or picking up after the kids."

Tom hears this response and speaks to the bed: "In my family, intimacy in the bed was reserved for conceiving children." This is the baggage that Tom needs to leave outside the door. He could not respond for the bed at this point, but Mary spoke up for the first time in this regard. Perhaps we can guess that baggage includes the passive model of woman who follows obediently as her mother and grandmothers before her did.

Mary says: "Tom, the children are a reflection of our intimacy, but I need to have those feelings and the physicality of that with you as well. I want to create the atmosphere that will encourage that, but I cannot deal with the golf, it is competing for your attention and sadly I don't think I can win this time."

It was an awkward moment as the couple stood there facing the bed and the practice tee. Then Tom spoke, "I hadn't seen it from your perspective before, but I agree."

We discussed the fact that what had been created in this shared space was not a shared decision. The bedroom is the domain of the "couple" where you literally must see "eye to eye" in a concerted effort to both maintain the eros needed to remain loving partners and loving parents, and to be the authorities for this family. This "affirming" dialogue was the beginning of a process for change in the home space, and a balancing of the family system.

Case Example: Eve asked for a consult for her apartment, a tenement railroad flat, where her living and work consisted of a loft bed above an office space. Her stated concern was that the mixed-use space might be complicating her ability to have a relationship. I arrived at the floor, and Eve greeted me at the entry to the kitchen, the back door. I asked her why she met me at the back door, and she answered that the front door was nailed shut. We went into the living room to look at the door and at the room in general. The door was nailed shut, but there was no apparent reason or need based on the layout or use of the room. I asked Eve to have a dialogue with the door.

Eve: "Tell me what you are feeling as the door that is nailed shut."

Door: "I feel like your protector, keeping you out of harm's way. The nails help insure that you will be able to do your work well."

Eve: "I do feel safer with you permanently closed. I wanted to do that a long time ago when I was growing up and my dad was abusive."

This understanding of the door as protector came from an old situation that was no longer relevant. Perhaps the abusive relationship with her father is also at the root of her difficulty in relationships. With the awareness of the door's statement, Eve might now have to ask other deeper questions about her living situation and begin to allow an intention to change it to emerge.

Case Example: I recently had a conversation about doorways with a friend who is a real estate broker. He indicated that ironically he has lovely house listing in a great location that has been on the market for over a year in a market that has been very active despite the economy. The irony is that the front door on this house is sealed shut. The listing photos and video do not depict the front door.

The owner, a single woman, indicated to the broker that although the house was built for her, and the door and entry were placed where she wanted it, the architect had ignored the energy flow (the Feng Shui) and the area of the front door was not right. Her decision to not use the front door was her solution. Apparently, the owner was interested in the Eastern concept of chi, which was not her background, but neglected the traditions of her family and the conventions of the area in which the house is located and of the people most likely to be purchasers.

A dialogue with the door might sound like this:

Owner: "I'm sorry you don't work well where you are. I will abandon you."

Door: "Why me? I serve an important function, isn't there another way to change the energy flow without sacrificing function?"

Owner: "It shouldn't matter to you. The way I live, the back door will suffice. Besides I do not like people on the street seeing into the house when the door is opened."

Door: "What about landscaping as a way of screening the inside when I am opened? I am the first impression people get when they approach, and I want to feel like an important part of the house."

Case Example: Susan, a single working woman, lives in a loft apartment divided into five areas: entry, living/dining/kitchen, bedroom, workroom and bathroom. Susan sees time and money as obstacles to achieving the kind of space that she would like to have.

Before coming to the city, Susan lived with her family in rural Iowa. Her parents and four siblings lived on a working farm run by her father and two brothers, her sisters worked in town but lived at home. Although her mother is a good housekeeper, being on a farm made it difficult to keep order. In addition, privacy, especially in the bath, was at a premium. You can see from Susan's reality plan that follows, her expression of frustration in not having things "together" in good repair and neat. These are the same criticisms she felt but never expressed while at home on the farm being cared for by her mother.

In the reality plan, we can see areas that are "cluttered, messy and neglected." Susan judged the dressing room as the "ego room" and the cracked mirror may reveal the limited view she has of herself.

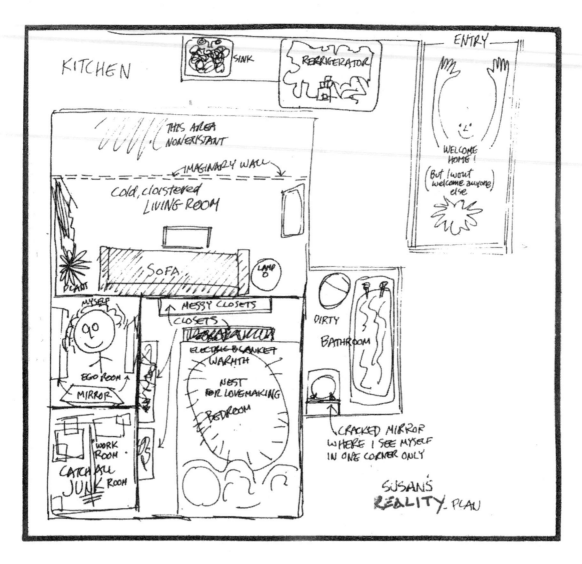

Susan: Reality Plan

The Ideal plan that Susan has drawn is clearly achievable without winning the lottery, but what needed to come first was the acknowledgment of her desire to be welcoming to others and to be self-nurturing.

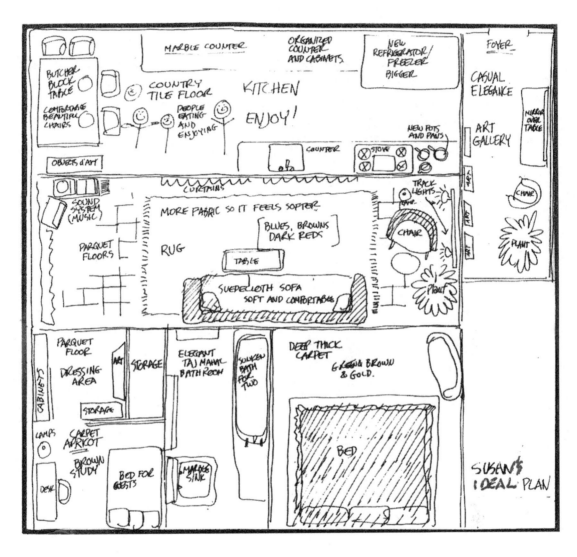

Susan: Ideal Plan

Exercise#13 Draw Your Reality and Ideal Plans

Take a large piece of blank paper and draw the reality plan. The plan should include front door or entry hall and the reality image of all your concerns. Is it muddy boots or long dull visits from the in-laws that start in this spot? It is not the drawing skill that matters here but rather the willingness to reach into your shadow, that part that is not politically correct, and allow it to be expressed.

Now draw the ideal plan including whom you would like to welcome at the front door and what you might do in that place to make it more welcoming. If you were an advocate for the door, what would be your fantasy drawing of the entry hall?

Chapter 11:
Blended Relationships

If you are a couple, issues may arise having to do with coming from different family and cultural backgrounds.

Case Example: Shana and Frank are both 35 years old and were recently married. Frank's family is from Northern Ireland and Shana's is from Iran. Frank has a successful career in law and Shana will be a homemaker, and they are expecting their first child. They have found a subdivision house in New Jersey. The house has a central hall entry with glass two stories high, making the stair to the bedrooms visible to anyone approaching the house from the street.

Shana feels uncomfortable coming down the stairs in curlers and robe, worrying that someone might see her. Shana's ancestors are from the Middle East, where women would have been protected from public view. The first level of protection would be the courtyard between the street and the house, and second would be by the shielding of bedrooms from public view.

Frank cannot understand the problem. His threshold of privacy is much lower than Shana's. In his cultural and tribal experience, the front door is right on the street. Open the door and the family is exposed. I ask the couple to each draw their reality plan (what is) and their ideal plan. When they are done we compare the two.

Here we see the issues that arise between cohabitants and their differing cultural backgrounds. Hundreds of books have been written about couples relationships and the need for communication between them that is necessary in order for the relationship to succeed. The impact of the couple not communicating their family and cultural differences will affect their living space and the impact of that will resonate throughout their daily lives.

The goal for all of us is the creation of balance and harmony in our homes. The balance between who we are as members of a family and tribe and who we are as individuals needs to be struck. The resulting sense of harmony will be reflected in the way's in which our homes are a source of regeneration for our pursuits, as individuals and as couples.

An example of the creation of balance in the case study with Shana and Frank might be on several levels: on the emotional level it is through the expression by Frank of his desire to protect Shana as a manifestation of his love for her; on the spiritual level it is through the creation of a private place for the family to be honored; and on the physical level it will be to modify the stair, perhaps enclosing it or at least shielding it from the street.

Of course, in seeking balance, the couple needs to take Frank's needs into consideration as well. His need to be open and transparent in the community, his need to be welcoming, and his desire to feel that his home is available to his child and his or her playmates are all of importance.

You can see how these diverse needs require not only communication but close attention in the design program. In an ideal world, Shana and Frank would start from scratch and arrive at a solution to satisfy both their needs.

Illustration- Shana and Frank's Reality and Ideal Plans

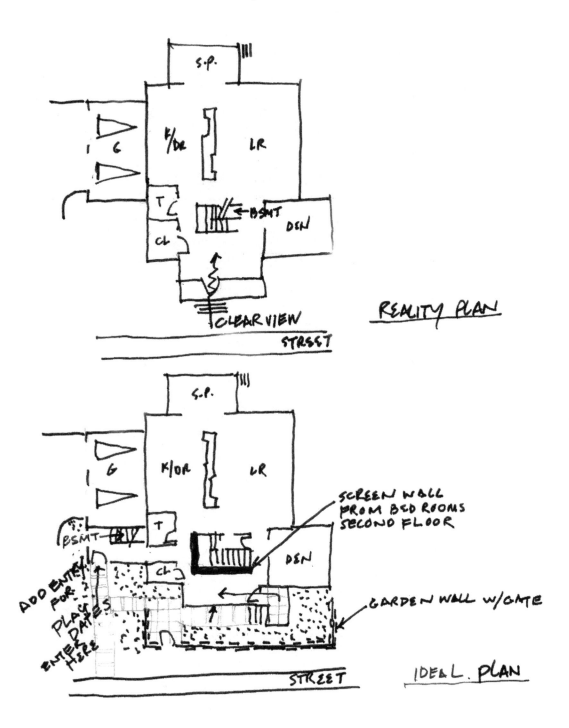

However, we are not in an ideal world and Shana and Frank may continue to purchase existing houses as they grow their family. The process they have gone through in adapting this first home to their needs will make it much easier in the future. There may be compromises in the future as well. The key is to make the effort to create the harmony and balance. The work of Section I is meant to be a tool to implement the process. There may be other tools that you evolve in the process. You can share these new tools with others; maybe we can begin a universal dialogue that leads to balance and harmony in each person's living space.

Do you see your home as a safe place, one that reflects your values, the values that you have experienced in your family of origin, and from a deep knowing place sense the connection of those values to the tribal culture? If the above is not where you are now, have you consciously acknowledged this to yourself, and at the same time acknowledged to your ancestors that you honor their way but you are moving on?

A Meditation

I visualize myself rising in light, working in space enough for my tasks, and resting in the quiet confidence that all my ancestors are accepting and at peace as they too share my home.

· · ·

Chapter 12:
An Inventory of the Spaces in Your Home

Now that you have had an opportunity to look at both the reality of the current space, and the ideal space that you envision, let's begin again, this time applying the following criteria: Is my home welcoming, energizing, nourishing, and does it fuel the reciprocity of life? Your home is already fueling the reciprocity of life in that it is either a positive or negative reinforcer of your strength or of your undeveloped side. Ideally, of course you would like to be reinforcing your strengths. As we take an inventory of home, I imagine that each space is a metaphor or an "out-picturing" of the way that you approach satisfying life's primary need for nurturing of self and of others.

Nurturance can take the form of food for a healthy body, or physical space and time for creativity and the exchange of ideas for a healthy mind. Both of these aspects of nurturance are active tasks. Then there is the passive nurturance of renewal, the space and time needed for reflection and creative emptiness.

Active nurturance can occur in the kitchen, the living room, and the home studio. Of these spaces, the kitchen is most central and the space most easily associated with nurturance. Not only is the food prepared there but contact is made during the preparation between cooks and observers. In earlier times, the kitchen was a part of the central space, or may have been the whole of the living space, with sleeping and bathing also occurring there.

The great room of the early settlers to the United States was a modification of that concept, only separating the sleeping and bathing. This great room was common in the rural areas of the United States and only became less prevalent in the mid 19th

Century, when urbanization began to dominate and dictate our house form. At the beginning of the 21st Century, the kitchen is once again a dominant space that offers much more than food preparation. It is once again central to the running of the house and the contact point for the family.

The living room has seen a shift in emphasis over time. In Western culture, up to the mid 19th Century, the living room was the family room and the parlor was the room for entertaining friends or casual acquaintances. Today, the reverse is the case, especially in suburban homes. The living room is for friends and casual guests, and the family room or media room is where the family relaxes.

I will say more about the seeming redundancy of spaces being built into today's homes in Section III. This redundancy creates larger homes at an expense to the environment, both in materials and in the energy required to operate the home. An intangible expense may be the effect on the family relationship as it appears to isolate sub-groups and limit their contact.

The home studio is another place of active nurturance. Of all the active spaces mentioned, this one usually ends up being the smallest. Sometimes it is a cramped, borrowed or leftover space. This may be justifiable based on the gathering of family and friends that occurs in the spaces mentioned earlier, but what about relative size in relation to the other rooms in your home? What are we saying when the space for creativity is small and often windowless? Taking time to reflect on the creative space, the home studio, is the only way to determine if there is a subconscious "squeezing down" of this space in order to "squeeze the life" out of it. How does this space compare with the way you feel in your body? Do you feel spacious, expansive, in touch with your breath? Or are you tight, restricted and out of touch with your feelings? Perhaps you haven't made the comparison of inner space to outer space and how your home is a mirror into the inner life. This inventory is a good way to start.

Find yourself a comfortable place, where you feel safe. This would be the place of passive nurturance referred to earlier, the place for reflection and renewal. If you cannot find that space in your home right now, I suggest that this would be a place to start to create change. Take the time now to create the space for reflection and renewal. I will describe how I see that space for myself, and you are invited to borrow or modify the description to meet your own definition, your own needs.

My Space for Reflection and Renewal

My best time for reflection is in the morning. On arising, I like to sit at a window and write. This practice referred to as "morning pages" by Julia Cameron, author of *The Artists Way*, works for me as I transition from the realm of dreams to the material world. For reflection of this kind, I find a seat at a desk or other writing surface. Once the work day begins, I am at a desk or in the car. I have made it a point of purchasing the most comfortable ergonomic chair available, one that has many adjustable features. During the work day, there are times when a break for reflection helps maintain the stamina required to get work done. Tilting back and raising my feet and gazing into nothingness for five minutes is a habit I have developed. In the evening before dinner, I find renewal sitting with my partner, my wife, in the inner space of our dining room, which has an upholstered seat. Sipping wine and catching up on the events of the day is a way of putting down the load of the day and preparing to enjoy a good meal and companionship.

As you can see from this description, there is nothing unique or challenging about my reflection spaces. What may be more difficult is the process of personalizing them, having them suit your needs, when you may not be the only user.

For the morning reflection, I prefer natural light. The window also allows me to extend my viewpoint, and although this writing is a form of active meditation I want to stay in the world as I come back into my body. The evening renewal space for half the year (living in the Northeast) is in a room with darker colors, with shades drawn, and warm indirect lighting. This encapsulates a transitional feeling between active awareness and sleep. These are important hours of connection between partners or between other family members.

For me distractions need to be limited, even music, unless it is carefully chosen and agreed upon by all, can interfere with the connections that lead to renewal. I have worked with many people who live alone and I have seen the same full range of needs as those as couples and families. One difference may be patterns that form as one transitions from one space to another. One such pattern I encountered is turning on lights or television before moving from kitchen to the dining area or from dining to living room. For this person entering a dark silent space for dinner after a long day of work is not pleasant. The key in this case is taking control of the environment.

A word here about relationship in general and as it pertains to home.

Martin Buber once said, "One should not try to dilute the meaning of relationship, relationship is reciprocity." We understand this concept of reciprocity in our relationship with others, the maintaining of a balanced give and take, to create harmony in the relationship, a way of learning more about ourselves than we would if we were not in a relationship. What about this reciprocal relationship with our home? What would be the balanced give and take? How can we learn more about ourselves through this "home relationship"? The balanced give-and-take with the home is very similar to that in the human relationship.

Awareness: Components including noticing what is good, and what needs attention, are part of it.

Mobilization: If there is something to be done, do it or arrange to have it done.

Contact: If there are areas of the home you avoid, make an effort to spend time there.

Check out the sensations, bring them to your awareness, and mobilize yourself to make changes. There is reciprocity in this relationship.

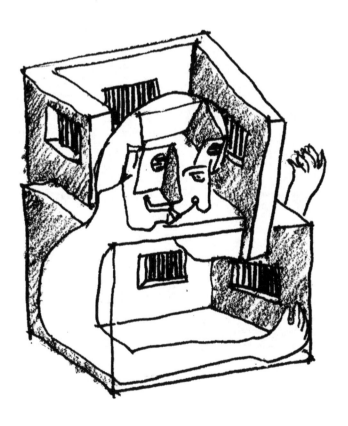

In Section III that follows I will discuss the need to align your principles with your practices. We will see that this may not be fully achievable in all stages of life, and that there is a need to be accepting of what alignments we can make, and not judging yourself for the ones you cannot make. This is a step in the process that goes beyond the family and ancestors, toward the new frontier, that place we have become aware of as conscious inhabitants of our home, EARTH.

• • •

Section Three
Where are You Going?

Part 1
Stage of life

The soul acts as a compass that is preset and at the same time changeable. There are constant changes that arise that challenge us to shift our direction. For example, we may harbor a desire to assimilate into a larger entity, perhaps for greater acceptance in order to achieve financial gains or to follow deeper, more emotional and animal drives for love and procreation, and embedded conflicted feelings may emerge, with the process. These are primarily due to the fact that though the soul may be predetermined and fixed, the "whole person" is not. We are more like a work in process.

On many levels we are constantly in a state of change. These changes often correspond to the stages of life: childhood, adolescence, young adult, adult, mature adult, elder. The ability to tune into change sometimes improves (if we let it) with age. In childhood, there is little tolerance for change and the need for transitional objects to bridge the gap is critical. Adolescence is all about change, but primarily on the physical and emotional levels. Young adults also find themselves in constant transition, moving away from dependence and toward self-reliance. Young adulthood is a critical period to prepare for perfecting the key to living since the voices that are prevalent are the old voices of parental control combined with the newer voices of peers, lovers, coworkers and so forth. Allowing one's inner voice to be heard in this period is a challenge. Often the living situation at his stage of life is transitional space as well, with hastily divided apartments and multiple roommates or small studios with thrift shop furniture. These transitional spaces are also the thresholds to learning about oneself in relationships and in relation to space.

The adult stage is really the first stage during which there is a sense of permanence and an opportunity to create consistency among the emotional, spiritual, and physical selves. Living with a significant other and sorting out similarities and differences as a home is being created is yet another transitional threshold to a deepening and fulfilling relationship.

Increasingly, transitioning from living in a relationship to living alone or in a communal situation is another stage to deal with. In this stage there is still a lack of consciousness in our society for the needs of the elderly. Needs such as accessibility, safety, and a feeling of self-esteem that comes from being able to take care or appear to be taking care of one's self are not given attention. Perhaps this is due to our desire to pretend that growing old only happens to others.

I know of elder housing designed in Vienna, Austria by architect Otto Wagner in 1900 that incorporated the needs of the elderly more than most being built today. His vision included hallways with user-friendly handrails, and ramps for wheelchair access. These simple accommodations took another 100 years and government legislation to achieve for today's elderly.

What happened in the interim? Initially, we may have had more emphasis on intergenerational living, especially as the global economy was affected by world wars, which created more interdependency. In the latter half of the 20th Century we have seen more affluence and with that a lessening of intergenerational dependency.

One outcome of this phenomenon is the separation of the generations, with elderly parents being cared for in private institutional settings. There are numerous external reasons for this imposed separation of the elderly. The younger generation is working, the elderly parent needs too much care, space is limited in the children's home, etc. What is lost in this separation?

I think of my own example described in Section I of my childhood when I was surrounded by my grandmother and aunts, and the richness that came with that. What is lost is not only the contact with and caring of the elders, but the language and the stories of the family culture. The recorded or written history of the elders still alive is easily attained today. Simple interviews or the collection of documents and photos that describe the family journey from distant lands to the current homeland are invaluable now and will only grow in value (emotional and spiritual) as time goes by.

· · ·

Part 2
Changes in levels of consciousness

There are two types of consciousness: the day-to-day awareness and the unity consciousness. Ken Wilbur expresses it in his book *No Boundary* this way, "It is the nature and condition of all sentient being; but we progressively limit our world and turn from our true nature in order to embrace boundaries—often the boundary established to define 'who I am' is that of the ego and identification with one's self image." Wilbur goes on to state that the remapping of the boundary to include the transpersonal is the process of going beyond the self image beyond the skin toward the unity consciousness.

One aspect of this new consciousness is bringing awareness in the form of a witness to the process of being at home. The process of recognizing all of the aspects of our true nature, including our ancestors, is encompassed in the process. This consciousness is reflected in your intention to change and take care of yourself and your immediate environment as a reflection of and catalyst for that self.

You may choose to respond to a new awareness, for example, that Western Culture in the Northern Hemisphere is using a disproportionately large portion of the world's natural resources, or you may choose to turn your back on it. It is a choice of profound significance at this juncture.

How did our ancestors do it? How did they survive the bitter cold and damp winters of Eastern Europe and Scandinavia? The first lesson they learned was that regional adaptation was essential. We can find examples of native building in cool areas, temperate areas and hot humid areas that respond to those climates. The cooler areas had compact dwellings tightly sealed against air seepage. The temperate area homes made less thermal demands and consequently there is more diversity and openness. The hot arid areas made extreme demands on shelter to reduce heat impact. More on the impact of climate on dwellings and regional character can be found in the work of Victor Olgyay in his book *Design With Climate*.

At this point, you may be saying to yourself, "Here comes the moralistic call to an austere life of self deprivation."

This is not a call for deprivation but rather a shift in consciousness toward intentional living, living that makes a connection between the choices we make in our homes from size to materials. Consider, for example, connection between the materials and their impact on the environment both in the manufacturing and the disposal cost including environmental cleanup. More can be found on this at the United States Green Building Council web site www.usgbc.com. This site will also have links to green building groups in your region.

Intentional living makes the connection between the abstract philosophy and the life style, between theory and practice.

Insight Into Action (for a change):

Do more in less space. Figure out what is really required with the result that you use less material, less energy to make the materials, and less fossil fuel required to maintain comfort in the home.

Use recycled materials. Choose materials that are manufactured from recycled products (usually plastic, rubber, metal and glass products).

Use sustainable materials. Choose materials for construction and finishes that are longer lasting and recyclable after they reach their life expectancy.

Use smart systems. Install temperature and lighting control of your interior environments that creates greater fuel efficiency .

The key word across the board is awareness. Gestalt practice teaches us that in order to become aware you must allow sensations within yourself to become conscious. These sensations are a reaction to your thoughts and to the environment and the those activities that affect your daily life.

With this awareness, can you hear your inner home saying, "I like it," or "I do not like it." If you do not like it, can you change it? If not, note the resistance and then locate it. Speak to the resistance the way you have spoken to other objects in the home in previous chapters. Perhaps the resistance is an old family trait that is holding on for dear life and does not understand the potential impact of the change you are suggesting.

Our task here is to deal with "home" as a tangible part of our psyche, and where you could not see the need for change or the resistance to change within you, perhaps you can see it out-pictured around you. This process of sensing and being aware of the sensations and making contact with your environment to create change is the essence of intentional living. The payback for the effort is priceless and enduring.

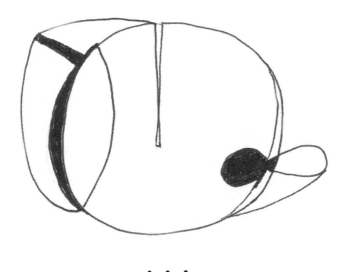

. . .

Part 3
Intentional Living

I believe that intentionality is the consciousness that converts sensory awareness into action in the external world, the environment. I sense it, I become aware of the sensation, I become energized, I mobilize myself, and I make contact with the environment. If the contact is complete, I am satisfied and I withdraw, and my intent will have been complete. If it is not complete, with a strong ego I will try again, recognizing that the journey from sensation to withdrawal is life being lived

I have set out four keys to The Art of Living Intentionally (TALI):

The first key:
Become aware of the changes that are occurring through the process of hearing your inner voice. It is up to each person to choose the way in which to discover the inner voice: for some, it is through dreams; for others, it is through meditation, or religious practice: and for still others it is the active repetition of the physical movement, active meditation that allows for an unself-conscious way in to hear the inner voice.

The second key:
Allow the changes to emerge and affect your relationship to the material world, spirit into matter as it were. If we are authentic in the moment, the reflection we get back should be in harmony with who we are.

The third key:
Create consistency between your heart, your mind, and your physical world. Matter confirming the spirit is the process that informs all action undertaken by this "authentic self".

The fourth key:

Perhaps the most important of the keys is to understand that perfection is not a key, in fact, it is an obstruction to the art of intentional living. So, when we look at the third key in this light, it is the journey that counts not the result. You may discover your desire to protect the planet for example and support the Sierra Club, NRDC, or other environmental groups, but not carry these actions further into your day-to-day living. Rather than feeling overwhelmed by the choices that you must still make, or critical of yourself for not making them, give yourself credit for the support you are already providing. Where there are inconsistencies between philosophy and life-style, note them and accept them as the challenges of the moment.

As you look around your home make a list with four columns. In the first column, note the inconsistency; in the second column place a check mark if you are okay with it at this time; in the third column place a check mark if you are not okay with the inconsistency. In the fourth column, note the potential solution to the inconsistency.

Check marks in the second column may indicate places where you may let yourself off the hook due to outer circumstances, but are committed to reevaluating at a later date. Those items that are checked in the third column need your attention.

Again, the first step is awareness.

The second step is to make contact with the environment, ie, check out reality to determine if there is a possible solution. Perhaps the expertise needed to determine the answer is not that far away or even costly. You may decide that the decision should not be based on savings as a determining factor, but rather the investment in a long range plan of energy independence and insurance in future comfort as fossil fuels become more scarce and costly

My own list follows:

INCONSISTENCIES IN HOME AND LIFESTYLE

ITEM	O.K. FOR NOW	NOT O.K.	POSSIBLE ACTION
Efficient use of oil		>	Upgrade to high eff. Boiler
Energy conservation		>	Improve window coverings
			Especially on north side
Energy Recovery Vents	>		Further evaluation of equipment
Alternate energy	>		Solar preheat for hot water
Electrical	>2(A/C)	>1(lighting)	1-Compact fluorescent bulbs.
			2-replace older A/C with energy star rated models
Water	>		Recycle grey water for irrigation.
Pool		>	Solar cover
Car	>		Look into hybrid pro/con
Recycling	>		Check w trash co.
Food waste	>		

Since I began this book, the cost of oil and gas has more than doubled. This means that the payback incentives have been reduced by half. In other words, what looked like a poor investment (from a purely economic point of view) two years ago is now good economic sense in addition to good environmental sense.

Exercise#14 - Inconsistencies

INCONSISTANCIES IN HOME AND LIFE STYLE

ITEM	O.K. FOR NOW	NOT O.K.	POSSIBLE ACTION

This same process can be used to address inconsistencies in other areas of your life as well. Physical health and nutrition are two areas that we frequently choose not to look at too closely. As long as they are kept in the background, there is an unconscious part of us that feels we are keeping potential issues at bay, but in reality we are creating an unconscious drain, one that will distract us from being in the moment, from being in life.

Think of the key elements that go into making a life, self, relationship, family, home, creativity. Home is the crucible that is shaped by and helps shape the others. It is time to be aware of the relationship, not superficially by expecting more out than you put in, but by first becoming aware of what is, and what shaped it. Is it of your own conscious choice? Are choices manifestations of rejection of family, or reflections of the strength of your family's values or representations of the unconscious following of the family way originally created out of scarcity and fear?

Whatever road you have traveled to the point where you are now, ARCHOLOGIE asks that you to take **a look back before you go ahead.**

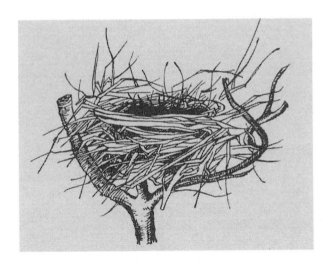

• • •

Bibliography

In order of appearance

Bert Hellinger Acknowledging What Is Zeig Tucker & Co. Inc.		1999
Rupert Sheldrake Presence of the Past		1995
Amos Rappoprt House Form and Culture Prentice Hall		1969
Robert Karen Becoming Attached Time Warner Books		1994
Fritz Perls The Gestalt Approach Science and Behavior Books		1973
C.G.Jung Memories Dreams and Reflections Vintage Books		1961
Dr. Steven Porges "Neuroception a Sub conscious System for Detecting Threats and Safety" Zero to Three		May 2004
Raechel Bratnick Awakening the Dreamer Society of Souls Press		2003
Ken Wilbur No Boundary Center Publications		1979
Joseph Zinker Creative Process in Gestalt Therapy Vintage Books		1977
Julia Cameron The Artists Way Tarcher Penguin		1992
Martin Buber I and Thou Scribners		1958
Green Building Housing Council Web Site www.usgbc.org		

Illustrations

Cover- Farmhouse in The Ukraine April 2008/Authors Living Room 2009
Inside Cover- Painting- Vincent Baldassano
All other drawings by the author

. . .

Postscript

In April of 2008 I went to Poland and the Ukraine to visit the homeland of my family and my ancestors. When I think of what my goal was, I realize it was not to find evidence of those who preceded me, but rather to experience the essence of the place and the things that made it home.

In the Ukraine I went to the Town of Podhacje where my family lived and the town my Grandfather Abraham left in 1894 to come to America. After experiencing the disappearance of the Jewish people and their culture from Poland and the Ukraine, I was surprised to find the Jewish cemetery and the Synagogue still extant in Podhacje.

The cemetery, which was on a high plateau overlooking the farmlands, was kept from being overgrown by the local goats, but the Synagogue that was nearby was not kept up at all. A tree grew inside through the roof and the stones of this once majestic structure were being taken for more mundane uses. Nevertheless, I was impressed with the size and strength of this edifice. I could imagine the worshipers milling about or using the community room on the lower floor behind the sanctuary.

The village square where the Jewish families lived up until the German invasion was where the marketplace was held and where Jews and Christians bartered and shared the fruit of each other's labors. The homes across from the market square looked very familiar; set back from the street with fenced yards, built of brick, they looked very much like the neighborhoods in Brooklyn where my grandparents had settled. I can only imagine my grandparent's excitement at coming to New York and seeing the paved streets and tall buildings. The comforts of central heating and running water must have made them true believers in the paradise called "America". As true believers, they must have chosen to forget their homeland, to blot it out of their memory, perhaps out of superstition believing that memory would pull them back. I remember.

. . .

About the Author

Jerome Kerner

There comes a time in life when it feels right not only to reflect on who you are but to share who you have become It is like a bottle of wine being saved for that "special" moment! Well what better moment than now? As an architect, I have spent the last 40 years helping people fulfill their dreams, needs, and aspirations for living and working space. During much of the 1960s and 1970s the creative process was mine with little mutual involvement by the client who usually acquiesced, and agreed to my solution. This is the way most architects still work. During the late 1970s and 1980s I placed alternate energy and energy conservation at the top of the list of design criteria. During that same period, there were government incentives for energy conservation and the client went along. During that period, I discovered I had an inner life, and a need to find my soul connections. Working with Dr. John Pierrakos, a Reichian therapist who created Bioenergetics with Alexander Lowen, and later Core energetics, I found aspects of myself that I had hidden away, that I thought were unacceptable. In the process of connecting with these shadow aspects, I unlocked a powerful source of energy and creativity. I believe the practice of seeing the hidden self and identifying that self in the home as well can free your energy and allow change to occur in your life and your living space.

• • •

NOTES

Made in the USA
San Bernardino, CA
17 February 2016